# Gardens of the Heart

# Gardens of the Heart

SUSAN CHIVERS & SUZANNE WOLOSZYNSKA

*Photographs by* PETER WOLOSZYNSKI

*Foreword by* PENELOPE HOBHOUSE

**Chatto & Windus Ltd**
London

First published in 1987 by Chatto & Windus Ltd,
40-42 William IV Street, London WC2N 4DF

Produced by Open Books Publishing Ltd, Beaumont House, Wells, Somerset BA5 2LD, England

Designed by Derek Cross
Jacket front panel designed by Humphrey Stone

British Library Cataloguing in Publication Data

Chivers, Susan
    Gardens of the heart
    1. Gardening 2. Celebrities
    1. Title II. Woloszynska, Suzanne
    635 SB 450.97

    ISBN 0-7011-3208-6

Typesetting by Wordsmiths, London
Colour origination by Columbia Offset, Singapore
Printed and bound by Royal Smeets Offset BV, Holland

# Acknowledgements

We would like to thank all the people whose gardens are described in this book for their unfailing generosity and enthusiasm which made our task so enjoyable. We are most grateful to Penelope Hobhouse for so kindly contributing a foreword and to Derek Cross who designed the book and was involved in it from its inception. Also, our warm thanks to Patrick Taylor of Open Books, without whose guidance, patience and resilience this book could not have been produced.

The naming of plants is a tricky business. It is a regrettable fact that correct botanical names are essential in any serious gardening book. The names in this book have followed W.J.Bean's *Trees and Shrubs Hardy in the British Isles* (8th edition) for woody plants; Graham Stuart Thomas's *Perennial Garden Plants* for herbaceous plants; and the *Readers' Digest Encyclopaedia of Garden Plants and Flowers*. In addition we have been able to benefit from more up-to-date guidance from recent books devoted to single genera such as Peter Beales's *Classic Roses* and Peter Yeo's *Hardy Geraniums*.

Susan Chivers and Suzanne Woloszynska

# Photographic Note

The general opinion among photographers is that gardens present their most photogenic character early in the morning or in the evening. From a purely photographic point of view this does indeed give atmospheric results. However, photography in full daylight produces clearer definition and thus, from a gardener's viewpoint, a more satisfactory rendering of colour and of plant effects.

All the photographs were taken with a Hasselblad using a 50 mm lens which allows plenty of subject matter in the picture without background distortion. I used Ektachrome 100 ASA on occasions when good blues were important and Fujichrome 50 ASA which gives particularly strong reds and greens. Nearly all the photographs were taken at F16 or 22 with a shutter speed of between 1/8 and 1 second. I would rather have natural plant movement resulting from the slow shutter speed which allows greater depth of field than use a faster shutter speed and have less depth of focus. A really good tripod was therefore essential when using slow speeds.

All film was processed at Push One, London. I have used them for 10 years and find them consistently reliable.

Peter Woloszynski

# Contents

# Foreword *by Penelope Hobhouse*

The English excel at being amateurs and adopting a 'throw away' attitude towards those things about which they care deeply. The 24 owners of the gardens described in this book are all amateurs in gardening, but well-known professionals in some other field. Their gardening activities, whether only idealistically creative or therapeutically manual or a mixture of theory and hard labour, remain only a small part of their lives. For each individual the need for a garden appears irrepressible; for each it is expressed in totally different ways. Unlike many purely descriptive books *Gardens of the Heart* inevitably explores the relationship between the owner and his or her garden. Many of the gardens are intensely private, the secret retreats of busy industrialists or statesmen, places where 'a soul's at ease', or if not at ease, at least alone and free to philosophise. These gardens are not planned for public display; there are no prescribed routes or rules for viewing as laid down by Louis XIVth at Versailles. As a result each garden is in some sense a frame to the owner's personality, and the text, amplified by superb illustrations, explores not only garden planting but also the owner's opinions on gardens and gardening. The gardens, as always in England, are diverse: similar sites are treated differently; similar styles, sometimes historical in context, develop along totally different lines. Jilly Cooper thinks that gardening is a middle-aged woman's substitute for motherhood. Penelope Mortimer believes it is an antidote to loneliness. Sir Nigel Broackes insists on a strong sense of order. Barbara Cartland finds her romantic woodland an inspiration for her novels.

This book can be enjoyed on two levels. The gardens provide appropriate, sometimes flamboyant settings for their owners, but that is not all. For any gardener or would-be gardener the descriptive writing provides thoughtful horticultural nourishment. The gardening styles are eclectic, perhaps less conventional than in gardens which regularly open to the public and tend to follow fashions or historical rules. In the last 20 years owners have become more aware not only of the history of gardening fashions but also the merit of matching a garden style to its environment.

The gardens in this book, on the other hand, frequently match the life-style of their owners, for whom the gardens are a part of their private as opposed to public existence. David Hicks has made a garden of pleached alleys and pergolas; vertical and horizontal lines softened by rich planting. This architectural framework at times looks inwards; at other moments the garden architecture frames a view of the Oxfordshire landscape. The essence of his garden is control. Lord Carrington's garden reveals the grandeur of yew shapes and the satisfaction of box-edged beds. Within this frame exciting plants complement each other and rouse the botanist's interest. Simon Hornby's carefully chosen plants are arranged in apparent disorder; in reality it is a stylish Jekyll-like exercise in disciplined plant association. Josceline Dimbleby disguises the straight lines of her garden perimeter with profuse planting to make a green oasis in Putney, while Robin Hanbury-Tenison uses the bleak landscape of Bodmin Moor as a backdrop to his gardening themes. These are just a few of the gardening responses made by the owners to their environment. Their gardens are full of interest and eloquently reflect the diversity of their makers.

# Jilly Cooper in Gloucestershire

JILLY COOPER WOULD LOVE to spend more time in her garden. Her writing and travelling commitments take up so much of her time that her obvious delight in gardening is tinged with a little guilt. She longs for the day when she can give it the hours that it deserves. As it is, she has to settle for odd times snatched between appointments or after long hours of writing.

Moving to Gloucestershire in 1982, Jilly Cooper and her husband Leo regard themselves as newcomers to the countryside. When they first arrived from London Mrs Cooper was very amused to be told by a neighbour that she must never have red in her garden and that red-hot pokers were definitely unsmart in horticultural terms. She ignored the advice.

The Coopers' 13th-century house lies on the edge of the lush Toadsmoor Valley. Its original inhabitants were monks from Malmesbury Abbey, many of whom are buried under what is now the croquet lawn which, says Mrs Cooper, may account for its excellent condition. The garden is by far the largest the Coopers have ever had to manage and after some discussion they have hit upon a fair division of labour. Mrs Cooper loves choosing the plants, planting and moving them where necessary. Mr Cooper is in charge of the vegetable garden, the water garden and general clearing. The garden was very neglected when they arrived and it has taken much time and effort, including some outside help, to get it into its present state.

In all the Coopers have 14 acres. Two acres are intensively cultivated garden which is divided into different areas each with its own character. In addition there are six acres each of magnificent woodland and of meadow. The meadowland slopes down to the river on the south side of the house. To the north the garden and house are protected by woodland from which there flow no less than five streams which are an immensely valuable feature of the garden. The soil is rich, free-draining limestone. To the west the garden is exposed to a fierce wind which blows from the Bristol Channel and is known locally as the 'Bisley-God-help-us'. Attempts to lessen its ravages have led previous owners to plant wind-breaks which include a long line of laurels. These have grown to a great height in the open and divide the meadow that lies in front of the house.

A sweep of gravel drive leading to the rear of the house is dominated by a superb cut-leaved beech (*Fagus sylvatica asplenifolia*). South of the drive an area of grass which backs on to the vegetable garden provides a good site for the decorative berry *Rubus* x *tridel* 'Benenden', one of the best of all dogwoods *Cornus kousa* var.*chinensis* and both green- and purple-leaved forms of *Cotinus coggygria*. North of the drive lie the woods of which Mrs Cooper is so fond. In the

Jilly Cooper pausing on the terrace between garden and typewriter.

spring they overflow with bluebells, wood anemones and wild garlic. A long shady border on the edge of the wood contains a variety of shrubs including buddleias, shrub roses, *Osmarea* x *burkwoodii*, *Senecio laxifolius* and the pineapple-scented *Cytisus battandieri* underplanted with *Hypericum calycinum*, *Osteospermum ecklonis*, bergenia and lady's mantle. This would seem to be the ideal site for hellebores but for some reason the Coopers have had no success with them. A gravel walk separates the woods from the croquet lawn. A pair of winter-flowering cherries (*Prunus subhirtella* 'Autumnalis'), one of Mrs Cooper's favourite trees, is planted at the far end of the lawn. On the west side of the house the drawing-room windows look out on to a wide stone-flagged terrace. This commands a magnificent view across the valley and down onto the garden. Below the croquet lawn, mixed borders lead from the terrace to a charming small gazebo. The main border is a marvellously exuberant piece of planting in which, during high summer, soft blues, pinks and greys dominate. Here is found one of the best wormwoods *Artemisia arborescens* 'Faith Raven' with especially finely-cut leaves; the white form of the meadow cranesbill; the valuable blue cranesbill *Geranium himalayense* x *G. pratense* 'Johnson's Blue'; several hybrid musk roses including 'Cornelia', 'Buff Beauty', 'Felicia' and 'Penelope'; the old Dutch woodbine *Lonicera periclymenum* 'Belgica' with purple flowers fading to cream; the wonderfully elegant *Thalictrum delavayi* (*T. dipterocarpum* of gardens) and many delphiniums. Among the more sophisticated plants in this border are scattered plants which give a cottage garden flavour – lady's mantle, catmint, yellow loosestrife, purple-leaved sage and tansy.

Beyond the gazebo a Victorian swimming pool has been restored and converted into a water garden. Mr Cooper has redirected two of the streams to feed the pool which is now planted with water-lilies. The surrounding boggy

Left: Beside the croquet lawn a carefully placed Chinese Chippendale bench is dwarfed by the woodland trees behind.

Right: Jilly Cooper's 'Mandalay' garden – an overflowing mixed border with shrub roses tumbling over the wall backed by woodland.

Roses and honeysuckles trained up rustic posts give height along the border and add to its cottage-garden exuberance.

ground is planted with many moisture-loving plants which include ligularias (both *L. dentata* 'Desdemona' and *L. stenocephala* 'The Rocket'), the corkscrew willow (*Salix matsudana* 'Tortuosa'), different forms of *Iris sibirica* and the huge *Crambe cordifolia* with its cloud of gypsophila-like flowers.

At the edge of the croquet lawn a newly planted yew hedge forms the eastern boundary of the wild garden. It contains substantial shrub roses (*R.* 'Frühlings-gold' and *R.* 'Nevada'); several kinds of philadelphus (*P. coronarius, P.* 'Belle Etoile', 'Beauclerk' and 'Virginal'), the insufficiently frequently planted *Elaeagnus umbellata* and the variegated *Acer platanoides* 'Drummondii'. A plant of special local interest is the curiously formed hazel *Corylus avellana* 'Contorta' which was first discovered in a Gloucestershire hedgerow. Another hazel in this part of the garden is the striking purple-leaved *C. maxima* 'Purpurea'. The wild garden, with its roughly cut grass and richly diverse planting of trees and shrubs, makes a perfect transition between the cultivated garden and the rural landscape beyond.

The vegetable garden has been restored by Leo Cooper and it remains very much his domain. It is now extremely productive and grows a wide range of produce. Here, next to the greenhouse, there is a special bed reserved for plants that are 'misplaced or misguided' – what Mrs Cooper calls 'an old plants' home'.

Mrs Cooper cannot remember when first she became interested in gardening. Growing up in rural Yorkshire, she has always loved the countryside and wild flowers. She enjoys walking in the meadows and woodland around the garden, marvelling at the variety of wild flowers that grow there. She loves to gather large bunches of cow parsley and include it in flower arrangements in the house. Her mother has always been a passionate gardener and thus plants and gardening have been important to Mrs Cooper from a tender age. It was natural to want to create a garden herself. In London she had a small garden which she still regards as an archetype. She would like to create a similar quality in Gloucestershire. A 'Mandalay' garden, full of secret places, overgrown and voluptuous, is how she sees it. In her perfect garden everything will be exuberant; plants will tumble over walls, climbers will obscure hard stonework; perennials will cascade on to paths from borders burgeoning with plants. All straight lines will be blurred with a quality of wildness. Despite several full gardening seasons she feels they still have a long way to go. Her garden is a romantic place and she spends much time trying to imagine how it will appear when mature. Her taste in plants tends towards old-fashioned roses (on which there is a great emphasis in this garden), lilies and delphiniums. She has a yearning to have an 80-ft swamp cypress instantly transplanted into the garden. Her pet hates are, revealingly, bedding begonias and bare earth. Nor would she feel happy with a formal garden – no pleached-lime alleys or topiary for her. Besides, she claims she is 'too chaotic' to cope with that sort of garden. However, despite her disavowals, it is obvious that a great deal of careful organisation and planning have gone into the restoration of their garden. Mrs Cooper attributes the planning to her husband and refers to her role as 'the muddler who just sticks in plants at whim'. She admits that she does not feed her plants sufficiently, but compensates by 'talking to them nicely' when she walks round the garden in the evening.

Mrs Cooper thinks that women make such good gardeners because of their maternal and romantic natures. 'What are gardens but children for the middle-aged?' she says. 'Unlike children they never answer back, never leave home and can be enjoyed throughout the whole of one's life.' The garden is certainly a priority in her life and provides a soothing relief from long hours of work. But it is essentially a private place and she and her husband have no intention of opening it to the public and are mildly suspicious of those who do. Although very knowledgeable about plants Mrs Cooper regrets that she simply does not have time to read gardening books. However, she has always especially enjoyed the writings of Vita Sackville-West. She is as passionate about her relationship with her garden as she is about her friends – 'Plants are like people,' she says 'it takes two or three years to develop a relationship and then they become really interesting.' Jilly Cooper's relationship with her plants is obviously developing into a life-long necessity.

Left: Dramatic contrasts of leaf and flower in the bog garden – ligularia in the foreground and *Rheum palmatum*, bronze fennel and *Anthemis cupaniana* behind.

Facing page

Top: The borders of the croquet lawn are softened with drifts of purple, silver and white.

Left: The sprawling rose, *R. x paulii*, makes a scented arbour for a Lutyens bench.

Right: A glimpse of the garden viewed from behind the converted Victorian swimming pool.

# Lord Denning
# in Hampshire

LORD DENNING IS RENOWNED for his prodigious energy. Since he was 80 he has written six books on his life and aspects of the law. It is only since his retirement as Master of the Rolls in 1982 that he has been able to live permanently in Whitchurch where previously he managed to spend only weekends and holidays. Today he takes great pleasure in country life and especially in his garden. 'It is our delight,' as he puts it in his book *The Closing Chapter*, 'to us, the most beautiful garden in England.'

Lord Denning was born in Whitchurch. When he was a child the house where he now lives was owned by two austere Victorian ladies who were often to be seen driving in a carriage and pair. Rigorously aloof, they never allowed their house and garden to be visited by the townspeople. Tom Denning, the son of the local draper, never imagined that one day he would own the house himself. He bought it in 1963 by which time he had been a High Court Judge for nearly 20 years and had recently become Master of the Rolls. Lord and Lady Denning's house is Regency, built in about 1820, and their garden is a glorious and tranquil setting for it. Lord Denning believes that the present garden was laid out at about the time the house was built and it has been his aim to preserve as far as possible its original Regency character.

The dominant features of the garden are water, trees and grass – all three combine to create a wonderful atmosphere of timeless peace. Lord Denning calls the garden informal and much to his taste. 'After all, I'm not formal, am I?' he says with an amused twinkle. The house lies beside the River Test, known to anglers as the finest chalkstream in England. Its waters are deliciously clear and friends are often invited to come and fish its native brown trout. This famous river, which runs across the garden, is a vital element in its character.

The garden and adjoining plantation and fields cover over 20 acres and are divided into several clearly defined areas. The most intensively cultivated part stretches along the river bank nearest the house and a 'wild plantation' with many shrubs and trees lies on the far bank. Wide walks, or 'rides', are kept clear in the plantation which provides a delightful walking place for Lord and Lady Denning. Beyond it there is a large expanse of farmland. To the west of the house lies a walled vegetable and fruit garden and to the east a three-acre field contains a plantation of poplars. Directly in front of the house there is an oval island – almond-shaped Lord Denning calls it. It was formed by digging a cut in the river, probably when the garden was first planned. It is the happy site of a magnificent collection of trees dominated by a pair of copper-beeches (*Fagus sylvatica*

Lord and Lady Denning on the
river bank with, behind them,
a swamp cypress (*Taxodium
distichum*).

*purpurea*) which Lord Denning loves best among all the plants in the garden. These trees are the central ingredients of the view from the wide terrace in front of the house across a sweep of lawn to the river.

A pretty Victorian cast-iron bridge spans the cut. Another bridge, an Italianate hump-backed wooden one, had regrettably to be removed when it became too rotten for safety. Lord Denning and his son replaced it with one of their own construction supported by old stones which had come from the great gateway in Lincoln's Inn.

Once the island had been cleared they decided to add to the existing mature trees. Several sycamores were removed to make room for some of their favourite trees. Now, twenty years later, these are fine specimens: a tulip tree (*Liriodendron tulipifera*) with its curious yellowish-green flowers in early summer and its distinctive leaves which turn a dramatic rich yellow in autumn; a weeping ash (*Fraxinus excelsior* 'Pendula'), now a large tree, with its leaves dipping into the water and providing a perfect nesting-site for ducks in the spring; a white willow (*Salix alba*) with its slender branches drooping at their tips and appearing silvery from a distance; and, very much at home, a swamp cypress (*Taxodium distichum*). Over the years the gaps between these have been filled with shrubs. There are a number of variegated hollies, viburnums (including *V. tinus*, *V.* x *burkwoodii* and *V. carlesii*), philadelphus, lilacs and several shrub roses (including *R. glauca*, *R. Moyesii and R.* x *cantabrigiensis*).

Lord Denning is particularly pleased that the old-fashioned character of the fruit and vegetable garden has been carefully preserved. A wide variety of produce is grown and the Dennings are entirely self sufficient in vegetables all the year round.

On either side of the lawn in front of the house large crescent-shaped beds frame a central area of grass. These are mixed borders with evergreen and

Left: Water and trees dominate the garden. Lord Denning stands on his island with an early-Victorian iron bridge in the background.

Right: The cut with its bridge. At the far point of the island is a large white willow (*Salix alba*). The gentle flow of the River Test is an essential ingredient in the garden's character.

Left: The new greenhouse with unusual Victorian staging which the Dennings rescued from a derelict greenhouse.

Right: One of the crescent-shaped borders in front of the house. Lady Denning's special Tree of Heaven (*Ailanthus altissima*) is underplanted with annuals and hardy herbaceous plants.

deciduous shrubs, herbaceous perennials and bedding plants. Lady Denning planted a Tree of Heaven (*Ailanthus altissima*) at the head of one of these beds – a decision she does not regret although it has grown excessively tall. A large *Phillyrea latifolia* ( a shrub popular in Victorian times which resembles an olive tree with handsome dark foliage) stands at the back of the border nearest the vegetable garden. Its glossy leaves provide a rich dark background for flowering plants. Other evergreens giving valuable permanent structure to this border are a mature *Viburnum rhytidophyllum* with its attractive fleshy and deeply corrugated leaves, *Skimmia japonica*, *Cotoneaster horizontalis*, laurel (*Prunus laurocerasus*) and hollies. Among the deciduous shrubs there is the one of the best weigelas, *Weigela florida* 'Variegata', with creamy edged leaves and pale pink flowers in early summer, as well as lilacs, hydrangeas and roses. Charlie, the full-time head-gardener, intersperses the permanent elements with annuals – tobacco plants, clary, godetias and petunias. Among the perennials are paeonies, irises, lambs' ears, gypsophila, michaelmas daisies and delphiniums. On the walls of the house there are a rampant *Clematis montana*, honeysuckles and a splendid *Magnolia stellata* which was a present to Lord Denning from Birkbeck College on his 75th birthday when he was its President.

From his library Lord Denning commands a marvellous view of the garden and island with its trees. He enjoys observing the rich wildlife of the river banks – where coots, ducks, herons and kingfishers are regular visitors. A favourite book in his library is John Parkinson's *Paradisi in Sole* published in 1629 and presented to him by the Law Society on his 80th birthday. Lord Denning frequently dips into it, finding immense pleasure in 'this speaking garden' as Parkinson called it. He has certainly made his own earthly paradise and, in addition, has worked, as he puts it, 'to make the garden of England a place where liberty and justice have grown and flourished more than anywhere else.'

# Sir John Gielgud
# in Buckinghamshire

FOR SEVENTY YEARS Sir John Gielgud lived in London. As a Cockney, he could not imagine living anywhere else in England. Indeed, in his childhood when his parents took him to stay with friends in the country, he found the green fields and woods of the countryside rather menacing and longed to be back in the safe confines of the city. Throughout his long career in the theatre he never had time to think about the pleasure a garden could give. Rehearsals, performances, travelling and the theatrical social whirl filled his life. At one time he even considered going to live in New York because 'he loved its vivacity so much'.

However, in 1973 the opportunity arose to buy the house in Buckinghamshire that is now his home. He was in a dilemma. He saw the house and instantly fell in love with it. However he was not sure that he would be happy in the country or whether he would become bored with the tranquility and miss his cosmopolitan life in London. A gradual transition of work from the theatre to cinema and television meant that he could now live outside London and not have to commute every day. He decided to take a chance and move out of the capital. It is a change he has never regretted.

Sir John's house is an enchanting brick and stone pavilion that was built between 1695 and 1710 as a service building for the main house at Wotton. It is suggested that the architect was Sir William Thornhill and the original garden was probably designed by George London who for many years worked for Viscount Cobham who lived nearby at Stowe. Sir John has lovingly restored the house and, latterly, the garden. In this work he has had the invaluable help of an extremely talented friend.

Luckily the plans for the garden are still in existence and so it was possible to study them and decide on a plan for its restoration. Taking on such a historic garden they felt that they had to get it back to its original splendour in keeping with its surrounding buildings. The result, after several years, is a tribute to their excellent planning and diligent hard work. Sir John is modest about his own contribution, but it is obvious that he relished this new-found pastime and has learnt a great deal about gardening. He enjoys walking in his garden whenever possible and takes great pleasure in 'pushing the wheelbarrow to the compost heap a few times a day'. This involves quite a lot of exercise as the garden covers about six acres.

The garden is composed of five well-defined areas. A semi-formal entrance garden, a parterre, woodland, a yew alley and a meadow garden. The entrance garden is a perfect example of nature ordered gently by the hand of man. Its

An elegant gazebo in the wood is one of Sir John's favourite places.

small lawn has apple trees with clipped box hedges surrounding beds of lavender and herbs. A wide flight of steps leads to a terrace with a small ornamental pool beyond which is the front door. Two buildings are found in this entrance garden: a derelict garage has been converted into a charming studio and a new orangery has been built. After several years it is now overflowing with exotic plants. Scrupulous attention to detail means that these buildings fit in perfectly with their surroundings. A low wall separates this first garden from the largest area of the whole garden – a parterre of approximately one and a half acres. A line of hornbeams (*Carpinus betulus*) has been planted along the wall and these eventually will be pleached. In the severe winter of 1982, two magnolias were lost and so a hornbeam alley, to add a formal edge to the parterre, seemed a fitting substitute.

The parterre lies to the side of the main house and can be seen perfectly from Sir John's terrace. He is lucky in having the grand double staircase leading from the terrace of the main house in his garden. It is the dramatic focal-point of the parterre. A niche under the top flight of steps houses a magnificent bust of Caesar Augustus. On either side of the staircase are the arches of the old orangery. Above each arch is a small gargoyle, all cleaned and repaired since Sir John took over. He thinks they were modelled on the original mistress of the house and members of her household. Each individual has been vividly depicted by the stone carver. Among them an apparently stern steward, a homely housekeeper, a jolly farm worker, a pretty maid and a short-sighted valet complete with spectacles. Sir John is captivated by them all.

When he acquired the garden he found that most of the hedges of the parterre had gone, leaving only one original segment. He supervised a landscaping and replanting scheme using both golden and green privet with stunning effect.

Left: The west side of the house seen from the grand staircase. The masks set into the arches of the old orangery on the left look down on the herbaceous borders round the parterre.

Right: The house from the south with a line of hornbeams fringing the terrace.

Looking across the parterre to the loggia with, on the right in the foreground, the lilac *Syringa* x *josiflexa* 'Bellicent' and, on the left, *Euodia hupehensis*.

Within each enclosure a stone urn on a plinth has been edged with a small bed of clipped box enclosing lavender and pelargoniums. Two Indian bean trees (*Catalpa bignonioides*) on either corner of the two segments nearest the staircase are among Sir John's favourite trees. The fountain in the centre of the parterre is new, replacing the original which had been lost. The two rubber decoy ducks floating in it are a caprice. A wide gravel path separates the lawn from the flower beds round the parterre and it is kept totally weed-free without resorting to weed-killers. Sir John dislikes the use of chemicals in the garden and none is used. These beds have all been renewed since Sir John arrived. He is fortunate in having the help of Vincent, his gardener, who has been responsible for getting the soil into fine condition. The garden lies on heavy clay and so top-soil has been brought in with peat and grit added. Good preparation of the beds means that now the plants are growing well and little feeding is required. Each bed has a theme; one white, one pink and blue, two yellow and orange, two are shady and principally green and two have mixed colours. There is an emphasis on subtle colour combinations and on those plants much loved by Sir John – delphiniums, lupins, lavenders, silver foliage plants but *no* gladioli which Sir John hates. The two shady beds contain magnificent collections of hostas and ferns. Between them, a dilapidated loggia has been restored from the original plans. It is a perfect place to sit and take in the elegance of the parterre and the grand staircase. Irregular arrangements of pots and tubs add an informal touch to its grand classical lines.

From the parterre, a path leads into the woodland area through a fine pair of wrought-iron gates, bought on impulse by Sir John in Paris. The wood is a complete contrast to the parterre. The trees are underplanted with informal groups of shrub roses (species and rugosas) and viburnums and lilacs. Sir John

23

finds the wildness and informality endlessly satisfying. 'I think that perhaps it is the most beautiful part of my garden,' he says. A small gazebo has been erected on a mound in the centre of the wood and Sir John is often to be found sitting there enjoying the shapes of the trees against the sky.

From the wood the yew alley can be seen through a gate in the wall. It is about 100 yards long and the yew trees have been left to grow unclipped. The effect is magical. Feeling strongly about the conservation of plants and wildlife, Sir John decided to make the fifth area of the garden into a meadow. Here wild flowers are encouraged to grow freely.

Not only the theatre, but all the arts have always meant much to Sir John. As a young man, he was a keen artist and imagined that he would make his career as a scenery painter. It was quite by chance that he was diverted into acting. When he was at Stratford one of his delights was to visit Hidcote and he has gleaned many ideas from it for his own garden. Today Sir John's artistic sense finds a new outlet in the garden. There is much evidence of a strong feeling for architecture and design. Not only are plant combinations and colours used to maximum effect but

Left: The new conservatory – overflowing with exotic plants.

Right: A classical fountain at the centre of the parterre – with plastic decoy ducks.

sculpture has been skilfully used. Most of the pieces are new to the garden and Sir John has enjoyed collecting them over the years. He feels that the balance and order apparent in the garden are products not only of his desire to create a garden to complement the house, but to mirror ideals within himself. He admits to being a very ordered person, always tidy and meticulous, to the extent of carefully folding his clothes at night before going to bed. He could not imagine allowing the garden to become neglected. He says, 'It would make me so unhappy.'

Work and through it, travel, still feature strongly in Sir John's life and take him away from Buckinghamshire at times. When he is abroad, he misses his home and garden more and more and looks forward to its peace and tranquillity. Having always led a wonderfully fulfilled life, Sir John feels that he is lucky to have found a new pleasure at this time in his life. His garden means a great deal to him now. In it he finds he has the time and peace to relive all his happy memories. 'I've done so much,' he says, 'Now I just want to think about it all.'

Top: A screen of limes and Spanish chestnuts separates the southern side of the parterre from the loggia.

Bottom: An 18th-century stone urn with the Grand Staircase in the background.

Facing page

Top: The herbaceous border at the west end of the orangery. Excellent initial preparation of the soil means that borders now need very little feeding.

Left: A fine wrought-iron gate leads to the informal yew alley. All the iron-work in the garden has been carefully restored.

Right: At the end of the yew alley stone greyhounds guard a gothic cast-iron bench.

# Penelope Mortimer
# in Gloucestershire

RECENTLY, PENELOPE MORTIMER WROTE a series of newspaper articles on expert gardeners and their gardens. One question intrigued her – why did they garden at all? Her contributors said they did it because it gave them pleasure; they had never bothered to ask why. Since Penelope Mortimer was bitten by the gardening bug she has asked herself the same question and has come to the conclusion that it has to do with the basic need to dispel loneliness. 'One is never alone in a garden,' she says. For her, working with living things removes the feeling of isolation to which all human beings are prone. She thinks too that the human spirit needs to express itself creatively and that gardening can satisfy this need. For her, that expression has become almost an obsession and something she still describes as 'trial and terror'.

When she returned to England from America where she had been teaching creative writing for several years, she bought a flat in London and a weekend cottage in Oxfordshire. Surprisingly, she found herself feeling more and more at home in the country and increasingly reluctant to leave it after weekends. Eventually she gave up London altogether. With this new-found rural contentment came the urge to create territory around her and thus began her interest in gardening.

With the enquiring mind of an academic and the self-discipline of a perfectionist, she started to research her new interest with all the dedication that is a hallmark of her writing. There did not seem to be anyone from whom she could get advice, so the first thing she did was to buy *Gardening News* and *Popular Gardening*; the outcome was the acquisition of an assortment of HT and floribunda roses but little else. Stumbling upon Robin Lane-Fox's *Variations on a Garden* and an article in *Harper's & Queen* called 'The Shaggy Garden', she found what she calls 'the vision I had been looking for'. So began her own gardening odyssey.

After the demise of the HTs and floribundas, she went into her 'nature' phase – growing camomile lawns and wild flowers with conservation in mind. This proved to be terribly hard work, especially after she was told by Miriam Rothschild that the wild flowers must be grown from seed in boxes and planted out 'in a precisely wild way'. A brief flirtation with the romantic 'Malmaison' type of gardening followed until it got out of hand, when it was superseded by an attempt to make a cottage garden – a period Mrs Mortimer now describes as 'growing weeds and saying "Oh, what a wonderful smell!"' Eventually she feels she became more discriminating and settled down to the sort of garden she is happy with today – one influenced by the Edwardian era, with some formality, a

Soft shades of pink and blue in the front garden of Penelope Mortimer's cottage.

29

wide and interesting selection of plants, the occasional statue and fine garden furniture.

Her garden covers approximately three-quarters of an acre. A small front garden informally planted with cottage-garden flowers like campanulas, paeonies, delphiniums and goat's rue (*Galega officinalis*) belies the sophistication of the rest of the garden beyond. It is full of carefully chosen plants, obviously selected by a connoisseur who still claims not to be a plantswoman. Originally the garden occupied a small area on the east side of the cottage, but Mrs Mortimer was able to buy part of the field behind the house and extend her garden into it. Near the cottage in the original garden, Mrs Mortimer has made a red border. Red plants do not, in themselves, particularly appeal to her but she regarded it as an exercise in precision and restraint; it would have been so easy to get it completely wrong. In it she grows two types of campion, *Lychnis chalcedonica* and the rarer *L. haageana*. There are also the purple-leaved ligularias 'Othello' and 'Desdemona', surrounded by oriental poppies of the deepest red. She allows herbaceous potentillas to straggle among the other plants and fills in any gaps with annuals such as dahlias, salvias and tobacco plants.

Nearby there is a long mixed border planted predominantly in yellow and blue. At one end, *Weigela florida* 'Variegata' associates well with the beautiful *Perovskia atriplicifolia* 'Blue Spire'. At the other end, a golden variegated mint seeds itself about the golden *Philadelphus coronarius* 'Aureus'. In this bed there is a splendid show of the pale purple tradescantia *T. virginiana* 'Purple Dome'. *Teucrium fruticans* is planted next door to a favourite hybrid perpetual rose 'Georg Arends' – a particularly effective marriage of soft blue and pink. Also in this border are the purple-leaved smoke bush, *Cotinus coggygria* 'Foliis Purpureis', a pink loosestrife, *Lythrum salicaria* 'The Beacon' and a favourite

Left: Penelope Mortimer behind the massive leaves of the ornamental rhubarb *Rheum palmatum*.

Right: Iris and alpine beds flank the path to the east of the cottage.

Part of Mrs Mortimer's 'library of roses' which is such a feature of the garden. The box hedge surrounds the vegetable garden.

astrantia, *A. carniolica*. Here too she has planted what she thinks is possibly her favourite plant of all, the Canadian bloodroot *Sanguinaria canadensis*, with its anemone-like white flowers in early spring.

From the terrace near the red border a gravel path leads to the potting shed and a small pool beyond it. In front of the potting shed there is a tiny, paved sitting area shaded by an old apple tree. Here, treasured blue Himalayan poppies (*Meconopsis baileyi*) and a *Magnolia stellata* grow in pots and the paving is fringed with *Dorycnium hirsutum*. In the potting shed is a huge collection of plants grown from seed. She has had some success in growing buddleias and wisterias in this way and is persevering with the lovely Californian tree-poppy (*Romneya coulteri*). She says that to grow things from seed is a compulsion and, ending up with so many plants, she 'inflicts a lot of stuff on the children's gardens'. Between the potting shed and the pool, Mrs Mortimer has built a rustic pergola and has smothered it with clematises. There is the large white-flowered 'Marie Boisselot', the deep-blue 'Lasurstern', the vigorous lavender-blue 'William Kennett' and the small yellow-flowered species *C. tangutica*. When she first planted her clematises she was surprised to find that they refused to grow 'pergola shaped'. It took her friend Rosemary Verey some time to untangle them and show how they should be properly trained.

The area of the garden behind the house consists of a broad sweep of lawn rising to the fields beyond. The lawn is broken up with specimen trees and shrubs and large island beds containing over 50 kinds of shrub roses. She calls them 'her great love for six months of the year'. When she first became interested in shrub roses, she admits that she bought them for their wonderfully evocative names. She was bewitched by 'Comte de Chambord', 'Souvenir de l'Impératrice Josephine', 'Honorine de Brabant' and 'Reine des Violettes'. With increasing

Top: The curving mixed border in the east garden – the rose 'Penelope' with clouds of *Crambe cordifolia* behind and *Astrantia carniolica* at the front. Further along the border the colour changes from pink to blue and yellow.

Bottom: Behind the red border a *Robinia pseudacacia* 'Frisia' rises above the red spikes of *Lychnis chalcedonica* and the bronze foliage of ligularias. The red theme is softened by the clever placing of other colours.

knowledge came many more and now they have been carefully arranged in beds according to their colours. Mrs Mortimer calls it her 'library of roses'. Among them all perhaps her favourite is 'Fantin Latour' with its delicate fragrance and blush-pink flowers.

In front and behind the horseshoe of roses is a collection of trees and shrubs, some of which have been planted to mark the births of Mrs Mortimer's eight grandchildren. There is a curious sycamore with leaves stained pink and purple, *Acer pseudoplatanus* 'Leopoldii' and a variegated poplar, *Populus candicans* 'Aurora'. There is also a special form of Norway maple whose new leaves are red, *Acer platanoides* 'Reitenbachii'. In the centre of the lawn there is a sweet chestnut and, a recent addition, an *Exochorda* x *macrantha* 'The Bride'.

Behind the cottage on the west side of the garden, Mrs Mortimer has made a small rectangular vegetable garden and surrounded it with a low box hedge that she moved from elsewhere in the garden. She has made it into a *jardin potager*, basing her idea on Rosemary Verey's at Barnsley House. It is divided by brick paths into small rectangular beds in which she grows a wide selection of vegetables and roses for cutting.

In such a small garden Mrs Mortimer has managed to achieve a remarkable balance between the romantic and the practical; she says she gardens 'with the same total concentration of a child at play'. Whether she is writing or gardening she applies herself completely – 'Whichever I am doing, I do it all the time – it is very exhausting and totally obsessive.'

Specimen trees and island beds of mixed shrubs on the west side of the garden.

# Professor John Hedgecoe in Essex

*A*N OVERWHELMING URGE 'to create something beautiful out of a potato field and a nettle patch' was the reason Professor John Hedgecoe gives for spending 22 years making his unique garden at Little Dunmow. As Professor of Photography at the Royal College of Art he has an eye for composition and understands how to create dramatic visual effects. These are the skills he has used in his garden. He says his interest stems from a desire to define space rather than to impose order on nature.

When Professor and Mrs Hedgecoe bought their house it was a picturesque farmhouse with a patch of garden at the back and the village cricket ground at the front. Over the years the house has been enlarged and the garden extended to cover six acres. Professor Hedgecoe started planning the garden with a clear idea of what he wanted to achieve but with no previous experience. Working on the basis that it must have sculpture, old stonework and trees and be principally green, he armed himself with gardening catalogues and set about realising his dream. At that time he had only a small amount of land on the west side of the house on which to try out his ideas. The first step was to make a boundary with the field beyond, using stone balustrading rescued from the Turkish baths at an old London hotel. Hoping to buy the field in due course, he left a gap in the balustrade to provide access. His first scheme was an exercise in perspective: a 30ft avenue of almond trees – planted with the lines converging and with each successive tree planted closer together to create an effect of distance.

Between the house and balustrade he laid a lawn. At one side of it he placed a sculpture by Bernard Meadows and in the centre a statue of St John beneath a mulberry tree. To the south of this lawn he made the first of his garden 'rooms', enclosing the space with a hedge of *Thuja plicata*. This small rectangle contained a large ornamental urn until 1986 when he changed the setting to accommodate a circular pool and a fountain. Although Professor Hedgecoe prefers to plant 'all the flowering things' away from the vicinity of the house, he decided to make a small 'patchwork' garden near its southern end. He built a round shell-covered house at the back of it with beds divided by brick paths and planted with herbs and small perennials.

Beyond the patchwork garden he laid out an enclosed rose garden in a star shape and this small garden contains an assortment of architectural memorabilia which Professor Hedgecoe acquired from the old Clapham Railway Museum. At the time it was made, the rose garden was the boundary of the garden on the southern side.

In due course more land was acquired on three sides of the garden. This

Professor and Mrs Hedgecoe behind a recently added fountain.

provided scope to create more 'rooms', avenues and vistas on a larger scale. Beyond the balustrade he planted a long avenue of the corkscrew willow (*Salix matsudana* 'Tortuosa') and built a pool with a grand fountain at the far end as a focal point. The willow avenue is now Professor Hedgecoe's favourite part of the garden. He says, 'The sun rises through the front door and sets at the end of the avenue.' The leaves of these willows appear early in the spring and are the last to drop. In winter, the elegantly twisted branches make a filigree pattern against the sky.

On the southern side of the willows, a narrow lake was excavated, with an island in the middle. The lake is now densely fringed with reeds, grasses, irises and day lilies. Many mature willows grow around it. At one time there were 120 different kinds in the garden but Professor Hedgecoe removed some when he realised that they were taking the goodness and moisture out of the soil and depriving newly planted trees. At the far end of the lake, a stone grotto overlooks the water. Inside, a serene statue stands beneath a canopy of 'stalactites' ingeniously made from the children's old nappies dipped in cement. At the end of the lake nearest the house there is a small and secluded paved corner enclosed by iron railings and entered through gates guarded by imposing stone eagles perched on pillars. Water is an important element throughout the garden; the careful placing of pools and fountains adds a romantic dimension.

To the south of the lake, a plantation of alders, planes and maples and a bank created from the excavated soil screen two simple green enclosures. One of these has a grass platform at one end and a life-size figure by Gabriel Cibber at the centre with a pair of sweet-gums (*Liquidambar styraciflua*) providing dramatic autumn colour. The other has a single walnut tree shading a circular seat. Beyond lies a long herbaceous border with traditional perennials such as wormwood, masterwort, sedums, phloxes, thalictrum, St John's wort and acanthus. Although he loves herbaceous borders, Professor Hedgecoe's idea has always

The avenue of *Salix matsudana* 'Tortuosa' with a fountain at the end.

been to produce a labour-saving garden. Even here, the border's informality is given an architectural note by the addition of a series of lime trees planted beside the border. At its top end there is a small vegetable garden, and close by a reassembled 12th-century tithe barn which was once part of Little Dunmow Priory. In front of the barn, a short canal is filled with rushes and water lilies.

Professor Hedgecoe thinks that people are usually too timid in the design of their gardens. He sees his own as 'being like a canvas which one can change at will'. For him, there must be something which draws the onlooker towards it to reveal another stunning view or surprising angle. On the west side of the lake he has put ten short 'wings' of clipped beech to frame an elegant temple containing a statue of St George. Further west, beyond the temple, an opening in a line of poplars reveals a large new area where a laburnum avenue leads northwards to a distant statue of a cardinal. In time, this avenue will become one long tunnel. Eighteen varieties of flowering cherry form another avenue at right angles to the laburnums. Within this space Professor Hedgecoe has designed an ingenious 'flag garden'. Six wedge-shaped segments of clipped *Thuja plicata* hedging are planted in a rectangle. The grass 'spokes' between them converge on a circular pool and urn at their axis. Each segment is planted with shrubs and small trees according to themes of colour, season, berry or scent. Professor Hedgecoe recalls that, to his horror, the 1250 shrubs needed for this scheme all arrived on the same day. Columns, stone ornaments and statuary add a classical note to this very original piece of planting. An evergreen hedge will eventually screen this part of the garden from the house.

Throughout the garden the large expanses of grass are kept immaculately mown. Professor Hedgecoe says that one day's work can make the garden look marvellous – 'Mowing the lawn is like having a new carpet put down.' He has laid cobbles around many of the statues, pools and specimen trees; they not only look smart but make mowing easier. Professor Hedgecoe is continually

The inside of the grotto at one end of the lake.

implementing new ideas. He would hate his garden to be like anyone else's and he is little influenced by others; he sees 'no point in copying'.

The garden lies on heavy clay and it is difficult to get things started. The ground is double-dug, filled with manure – hundreds of tons of pig manure have been put in over the years – and resealed with clay which allows the roots to break through when the subject has matured. Professor Hedgecoe frequently moves trees three or four times until both they and he are happy with their situation. Mrs Hedgecoe has got used to finding that parts of the garden have disappeared or reappeared in another guise elsewhere. Professor Hedgecoe likens his restless creativity to 'building sets and changing them'. He also likes to change the shape of existing trees, especially the weeping ones. He used to be so fond of these but now finds that it is impossible to mow under them. So he has clipped a weeping pear (*Pyrus salicifolia* 'Pendula') into a drum shape and is training the mulberry on the lawn into an umbrella shape. 'There is no year in which something has not been added or changed,' he says. He loves what he calls 'super leaves' and the effect of 'green on green on green', taking great delight in 'putting in a stick and watching it grow into a tree'. For all his hard work and patience, he is unsentimental about his garden and would be quite happy to start again elsewhere, ideally with 20 or 30 acres in which to indulge his passion.

Professor and Mrs Hedgecoe (who is also a photographer) often use their house and garden as locations in their work. Perhaps this accounts for Professor Hedgecoe's professional approach and meticulous standards in the garden. This is not a traditional flower-lover's garden but a glorious composition of interlinking spaces, defined by trees and hedges, and made dramatic by the careful placing of statues, fountains, pools and architectural *objets trouvés* – an exercise in line and perspective on the grand scale. There is no doubt that the garden bears the stamp of its creator's determined individuality.

# A.L.Rowse
# in Cornwall

DR A.L.ROWSE'S GARDEN at Trenarren by St Austell Bay forms a spectacular amphitheatre with the sea as its backdrop. If ever a garden was determined by its natural setting this is one. Doubly blessed with protecting hills to the north and the gentle Cornish climate, this is an ideal setting for the magnificent rhododendrons which emphatically take centre stage.

In 1612 the Hext family came to Trenarren from Devon and Somerset and built their first house on a sheltered slope in the valley. The present house was built in 1805, 'the year of Trafalgar' as Dr Rowse is quick to remind one. The position chosen was an especially beautiful one and the Hexts started to lay out the garden shortly after the new house was built. They planted many of the rhododendrons which today contribute much to the structure of the garden. They have grown to a great size and here in Cornwall they seem quite at home and fit in to the surrounding countryside with great naturalness.

The house is built of grey Cornish granite but the south front is faced with beautiful Pentewan stone, ashlar cut, which reflects the light and gives out subtle colours. This side of the house provides a particularly warm site. Here *Sophora tetraptera* flourishes with its finely cut pinnate leaves and decorative trumpet-shaped flowers in the winter. It is one of many Australasian plants in the garden, which include senecios, olearias, hebes and callistemons. Here they find a micro-climate perfectly to their liking and grow with exceptional vigour. From the terrace that runs along this side of the house a soft scoop of lawn falls away to meet a massive wall of vibrant cerise rhododendrons, some of which are over 150 years old. Above them one catches glimpses of the shimmering sea out in St Austell Bay. Dr Rowse says that the garden owes everything to the Hext family who first laid it out. Much of their original scheme survives. The species rhododendrons which now dominate the giant borders that fringe the lawn date from this period. In addition they planted many clumps of bamboo, laurels and ilex which must have provided valuable wind-shelter for less robust plantings. One of the plants here is among Dr Rowse's favourites – both for its intrinsic beauty as well as for its historical associations with the Elizabethan Age. This is Winter's bark, *Drimys winteri*, which grows in Cornwall to quite exceptional size. It is named after Captain William Winter, Sir Francis Drake's second-in-command who turned back in 1578 from the Straits of Magellan where the shrub grows naturally. Trengwainton, also in Cornwall, has one of the largest specimens in England of this handsome evergreen shrub with its resplendent glossy foliage.

Throughout the 33 years that Dr Rowse has lived at Trenarren he has

The house faces a sweep of massive rhododendrons –primulas cover the slope.

constantly made additions to the planting. Notable among these are a profusion of camellias – both japonica and reticulata – and magnolias and azaleas. The planting is on a grand scale – anything less in such a magnificent setting would seem wrong. Nonetheless there is some underplanting of a more intimate kind. In the spring carpets of primulas, cyclamen and anemones spread themselves beneath the shrubs. Spring comes early in this part of England and at Trenarren it is the most dramatic moment of the gardening year. Dr Rowse claims that 'gardening in Cornwall is so easy – I just pop bits in and they grow.' Indeed he has propagated many plants without the aid of greenhouse or coldframe and plants cuttings direct into the ground with rarely a failure. His successes include *Pieris formosa* var.*forrestii*, *Callistemon citrinus* (which in less favoured areas is deemed a shrub for the greenhouse) and a fine eucryphia.

Beyond the rhododendrons and magnolias flanking the central amphitheatre there are glades of chestnut, fern-leaved beech (*Fagus sylvatica asplenifolia*) and Scots pines. Each part of the garden has its identifying name. The most sheltered part is 'The Manciple's Patch', named after a holder of that office at All Souls' College, Oxford, of which Dr Rowse is an Emeritus Fellow. The Manciple helped to plant this bed which contains many tender camellias, magnolias and hellebores. It is here that Dr Rowse has planted the sub-tropical *Echium bourgeanum*, a native of the Canary Islands, that came from Tresco in the Scilly Isles. It settled down quite happily and soon was self-seeding prolifically. However, it seems to have suffered a setback in the cruel winter of 1985/6 but there is every hope that seedlings will spring up again. Beyond the central bank of rhododendrons lies 'The Paddock'. This had been a flower garden but is now an exotic glade fringed with mimosas (*Acacia dealbata*) which sow themselves with abandon. Behind is 'The Jungle', a densely wooded slope which rises to a fine stand of Scots pines at the brow of the hill.

Dr Rowse has added many shrubs to the original plantings of hybrid rhododendrons. Here, a blood-red camellia and *Magnolia* x *soulangiana* 'Alba Superba' reflect the spring sunshine.

Left: A magnificent white form of *Rhododendron arboreum* dominates one side of the garden. From here the sea can be glimpsed over the bank of rhododendrons.

Right: From this vantage point in front of the house Dr Rowse can enjoy his garden and the Cornish landscape which has been so important to him throughout his life.

Since his retirement (if one can think of a man who so tirelessly writes books and lectures around the USA as being retired) Dr Rowse has extended the garden informally into the woodland to the west. 'The Wilderness' gives him much satisfaction. Here immense thickets of brambles were cleared and there are now many daphnes, olearias and hydrangeas – which last, says the Doctor, 'grow like weeds here'. In this quiet place of dapppled sunlight and birdsong he likes to walk and plan his writing while tidying the meandering paths. His housekeeper Phyllis possesses, among others, two exceptional skills. She makes superlative Cornish pasties and knows how to build a bonfire. In a place rich with ash from one of her bonfires is a pocket handkerchief tree (*Davidia involucrata*). The extraordinary pale bracts of this tree are seen fluttering aloft in early summer. To the south is 'The Tennis Court Garden' which is a remarkably ingenious example of what can be made from a disused hard court. Dr Rowse has simply made holes in the surface and stuck in cuttings. Nature has done the rest and it is now a large expanse of trees and shrubs dominated by a mature balsam poplar (*Populus balsamifera*). Here too another Australasian plant, *Griselinia littoralis*, from New Zealand, grows happily. This evergreen shrub, with its attractive wavy-edged leaves, adds a note of distinction to any planting scheme. One specimen at Trenarren is among the largest in Cornwall.

As a child Dr Rowse used to spend hours sitting on the wall outside Trenarren. At this time both house and garden were sadly deserted. It was his dream to live there and bring it back to life. His father, a china clay worker, had great faith in his son's abilities. One day he told his wife that no doubt their son would eventually live at Trenarren but that he himself would not live to see it. This was indeed the case and now Dr Rowse seems thoroughly in his element in this remarkable Cornish garden. 'Sometimes it overwhelms me with its beauty. Happily it does not distract me; it simply encourages me onward.'

# Sir Peter Parker
# in Oxfordshire

SIR PETER PARKER FIRMLY BELIEVES that everyone has an element – earth, fire, air or water – which remains an influence throughout life. He feels that his element is water and his wife's earth: a fortunate combination for the creation of their garden at Minster Lovell.

Until the Parkers bought Manor Farm 12 years ago, it was in a semi-derelict state and under threat of being turned into a hamlet of 'desirable' homes. Thanks to the Parkers' intervention, the farmhouse, its fine barns and outbuildings have been sensitively restored and they have created a garden that beautifully complements the idyllic setting. Situated near the River Windrush, the 15th-century farmhouse was built on the site of the Roman road from Wychwood Forest to Witney. Behind Manor Farm stands the church whose graveyard backs immediately onto the Parkers' house, and behind that again the ruins of a 15th-century manor house built by the Lovell family – a reminder of the historic past of this peaceful corner. Sir Peter says that they have frequently dug up archaeological 'things' around the garden. He obviously takes great pleasure in the restoration and upkeep of the ancient buildings that are such a vital feature of the garden.

Before coming to Minster Lovell, the Parkers' only gardening experience had been in a tiny London garden which, according to Sir Peter, 'never had a hope'. Far from being daunted by the prospect of making a large garden, Sir Peter says that his wife had 'the gift of vision' which she applied equally to the planning of the garden and the restoration of the house. Sir Peter feels that he is not an instinctive gardener and that his contribution to the garden 'is in the role of Caliban'. With Lady Parker's ability to visualize the effect of new planting and Sir Peter's love of organization and a good sense of detail, the garden has evolved over the years. They have worked with the precept that 'no part of it should be isolated, with each flowing into the next'. Although each part of the garden has its own character none is abruptly cut off from the rest.

This principle is found at the entrance where the drive is edged with a river of shrub roses including 'Constance Spry', 'Président de Sèze' and 'Bonn'. A small croquet lawn behind is almost hidden by the profusion of flowers of the 'Nevada' roses on the other three sides. On the far side of the lawn, a pergola is hung with the creamy-white trusses of the rose 'Bobbie James'. At the end of the lawn a small herb garden with a sundial stands in the shelter of an old barn. The drive sweeps into a large gravel yard, the centre of a ring of ancient barns and other outbuildings. The house stands to one side of the barns and the Cotswold stone makes a perfect foil for what Sir Peter describes as 'the heraldic red' of the

Sir Peter and Lady Parker
under a pergola covered with
the rose 'Bobbie James'.

climbing rose 'Altissimo' and richly coloured pansies beneath. Near the front door Moroccan broom (*Cytisus battandieri*) makes a satisfying combination with *Cotoneaster horizontalis*, hellebores and rue. On the far side of the door, a shaded sunken area is planted with an assortment of ferns, hellebores, hostas and a lovely pink masterwort (*Astrantia carniolica* 'Rubra'). One of the ferns grows in a curious spiral shape and particularly intrigues Sir Peter. On the wall behind, the rose 'Madame Caroline Testout' grows next to a *Hydrangea petiolaris*. The low wall enclosing this little green oasis is draped with ivy and aubretia.

From the front door a cobble and stone-flagged path leads to two beds, one planted with paeonies, philadelphuses, a *Spiraea* x *arguta* and *Rosa macrantha* 'Raubritter' which rambles over the path. The other contains delphiniums, irises, yellow shrubby potentillas, lupins, masterwort, veronicas, heuchera, eryngiums, a white *Campanula persicifolia* and cranesbills. Various plants have spread themselves over the path and these include thymes, pinks, golden marjoram and plenty of lady's mantle.

The large lawn beyond is divided by a single step half way down. On the lower side, old apple trees cast pools of shade and the rugosa rose 'Frau Dagmar Hastrup' planted under one of them now forms a full skirt about it. Another tree is draped with the climbing rose 'Félicité et Perpétue'. On the upper half of the lawn, Lady Parker has laid out a 'rose ring'. This idea evolved from her wish to break up the blank lawn and to allow the roses enough room to develop their natural shape. 'I tend to plant too closely,' she says. Among the many shrub roses old favourites include 'Souvenir de la Malmaison', the bourbons 'Madame Isaac Péreire' and 'Madame Pierre Oger', the purplish rugosa 'Roseraie de l'Hay' and the fine alba 'Königin von Dänemark'. This is now one of the Parkers' favourite features of the garden and although it goes against his instinct for order, Sir Peter confesses that he likes 'the untidiness of the roses'. It was his idea

Left: An old barn shelters one end of the herbaceous border. The soft colours complement the Cotswold stone.

Right: Looking up the border where the roses 'New Dawn' and 'Constance Spry' are trained against the wall of the barn. Lady Parker's intention has been to create an effect that is 'light in weight and colour'.

46

Left: The front of the house seen from beneath an old apple tree on the lower lawn. In the foreground *Rosa macrantha* 'Raubritter' cascades over the path.

Right: Beside the front door a sunken area is filled with shade-loving plants. The rose 'Madame Caroline Testout' and *Hydrangea petiolaris* cover the wall behind.

to plant a variety of hollies as a backdrop to the 'rose ring'. He adores sharp-edged plants and particularly the spikiness of holly leaves. Sir Peter has invented names to identify different parts of the garden; appropriately, he calls this small plantation 'Hollywood'. Behind it, a wood of chestnuts and oak, and a fine Himalayan birch (*Betula jacquemontii*), marks the boundary of the garden on this side.

On the lower lawn the Parkers have recently made a curving alpine bed in front of what they call 'The White House' – once the outside privy. The rockery is home to an assortment of thymes, saxifrages, and arabis. Sir Peter likes the structured form of dwarf conifers and evergreens and he has managed to 'smuggle in' a few about the garden. To one side of 'The White House', white annual mallows (*Lavatera trimestris* 'Splendens Alba') grow near the magnificent Californian tree poppy (*Romneya coulteri*). The white theme of this area includes a *Clematis spooneri* and *Solanum jasminoides* 'Album' which will soon ramble over 'The White House'. Alongside, a new white bed is planted with a mixture of shrubs, 'White Cockade' roses and perennials including carnations and astilbes, pansies, hostas and one of Lady Parker's favourite plants, *Dicentra spectabilis* 'Alba'. Lady Parker's lovely herbaceous border lies in the shelter of a barn at the far side of the lower lawn. She says that she wanted it to be 'light in weight and colour' in contrast to the 'coarser' beds of paeonies and lupins by the front door. The colours in this border were chosen to harmonize with the roses 'New Dawn' and 'Constance Spry' which grow up the wall of the barn behind. The blue spires of delphiniums, *Campanula persicifolia* and catmint mingle with the yellows of a pale achillea, verbascums and clumps of shrubby potentilla – which Lady Parker describes as 'the yeomen of the garden – sturdy and colourful'. Pinks, carnations, violas and cranesbills echo the colours of the roses and *Acanthus spinosus*, Solomon's seal, and Japanese anemones provide leaf contrast. *Stachys lanata*

Facing page

The new upper pond with an old dovecote behind. To one side, the beams of an old outbuilding provide an 'instant' pergola by the lower pool.

'Silver Carpet' ensures good ground cover in any gaps and lady's mantle spills over onto the grass at intervals. Lady Parker is keen on effective plant associations and she moves things constantly until the effect she has visualised is achieved.

On the eastern side of the house, a raised terrace is fringed with lavenders and miniature roses. Here the walls provide a sheltered spot for the roses 'Buff Beauty' and 'Königin van Dänemark' and the delicate yellow lanterns of *Clematis tangutica*. Immediately below the terrace the rough stone floor of an old farm building is known as 'Thymes Square'. Different kinds of thyme are planted in cracks accompanying 'Iceberg' roses, a white cranesbill, arabis and foxgloves. The doors of Sir Peter's study, or 'hut' as he calls it, open onto this little square.

From here, the garden extends southwards into a large orchard with the church and ruins behind. The west-facing wall of the orchard has a hedge of *Rosa glauca* planted along its length – 'to catch the evening sunlight', Lady Parker says. The rough stone floor of what was once a farm building is covered with a tapestry of self-seeding plants. Here are evening primroses, thymes, alpine strawberries and dark purple violas. The climbing rose 'Kathleen Harrop' coils up a simple archway – known as 'The Pearly Gate' – which leads out of this part of the garden.

The great tithe barn beyond the orchard has Saxon origins and Sir Peter has ensured that it retains its original character. Today, however, it is used for barn-dances rather than for storing corn. Nearby, Sir Peter has had a water garden made. He has always loved the sea and having chosen to live in a place which could not be further from it, he decided that water was an absolute necessity in the garden – 'it doubles the pleasure with its delightful reflections.' Two pools were excavated in 1986. The first is a round pond which makes a perfect foreground for a fine old dovecote dominating this part of the garden.

Part of the Rose Ring on the upper lawn.

The Parkers have recently started planting the edge of the pond with hostas, astilbes, ligularias, candelabra primulas, kingcups, irises and a flowering rush, *Butomus umbellatus* which has pretty umbels of rose-pink flowers. Sir Peter has set a stone seat in the wall by the pool and this is now a favourite spot for him to sit and read. Steps lead down to the second pool through another archway known as 'The Golden Gates' – aptly named as it is entwined with the yellow flowers of the roses 'Leverkusen' and 'Highfield' and the tendrils of the golden honeysuckle *Lonicera japonica* 'Halliana'. The lower pool is rectangular and is set in a frame of cobbles and old stone. Alongside, the roof and front wall of a barn have been removed. The remaining wooden supports now serve a dual purpose. First, they allow an uninterrupted view over the countryside from the garden above and secondly they provide an 'instant' pergola. Sir Peter loves architectural plants and beneath the pergola's outer wall *Helleborus corsicus* has been planted. A variety of plants chosen for their strong form are grown at the base of the pergola's supporting timbers. These include *Acanthus spinosus*, plume poppies (*Macleaya cordata*), angelica and bronze fennel. At one end of the pergola there is a piece of gnarled May tree which resembles the sprawled figure of a fallen soldier. Sir Peter calls it his 'crusader'. At the other end, he has put a Japanese lantern or *toro*, traditionally used in the tea ceremony.

The Parkers lead very busy working lives and treasure every moment spent in their garden at weekends. Sir Peter says that his wife gardens 'with all the passion of a convert' while, for him, the garden is a place for quiet reflection and self-discovery. After 12 years, Lady Parker says that it is developing into a civilised jungle and that the pleasure of gardening is 'exploring the jungle'. For Sir Peter, the pleasure is 'the timeless dimension and sense of continuity of the place'. All in all, it is a quite unusually satisfying garden in which a great range of good plants flourishes in a setting of wonderful charm.

The drive is edged with shrub roses. The house, church and ruins can be seen beyond the croquet lawn.

50

Top: 'Thymes Square' in the foreground with the orchard beyond.

Bottom: The cobbled floor of what was once a cowshed is now covered with self-sown plants. In the foreground the rose 'Kathleen Harrop' adorns a simple archway.

# Josceline Dimbleby in Putney

FOR JOSCELINE DIMBLEBY, gardening began in a window-box of her first London flat. Now she has two gardens; one in Putney where she, her husband David and their three children live for most of the time – and one in Devon where they spend their holidays. The Devon garden has to be left largely in the care of a local gardener, although Mrs Dimbleby was responsible for its initial planting. The garden at Putney, however, is in her sole care. She says that this garden has evolved in an unplanned, haphazard way and her gardening knowledge has come from experience rather than from reading. As a cookery writer she likes to experiment and to break the rules, and avoids specialist books which she finds limiting to the imagination; so it is with her gardening.

Mrs Dimbleby grew up with the idea of becoming a professional singer, and after school went on to train at the Guildhall School of Music. A large *Magnolia* x *soulangiana* 'Alexandrina' in her front garden reminds her of those days each time she looks out of her sitting-room window. It was given to her by her singing teacher and has become especially precious since she died. Now a 10ft tree, it serves as a permanent reminder of the giver and is a good example of Mrs Dimbleby's belief that trees and shrubs make the best presents. The small front garden has a high hedge of the roses 'Albéric Barbier' and 'Albertine' and a lawn with the magnolia in the middle. Beside the hedge there is a seat/sculpture made by Mrs Dimbleby's brother-in-law, Nicholas Dimbleby. Outside the front door there are 'Iceberg' roses in pots. Mrs Dimbleby put them there so that they may 'give off their delicate scent in the evening as you brush past them'.

At the back of the house, the garden is typical of many town gardens: a rectangle of about 100 by 60ft. However, it is very much her own creation and shows her preference for 'an overgrown garden full of secret places, but not out of control'. It is reached through french windows from the drawing-room and the immediate impression is one of lushness with nearly all nearby buildings obscured by a screen of trees and shrubs. The central lawn has tree and shrub borders on either side. These have been densely planted and curve inwards towards each other two-thirds of the way down the garden, forming a narrow isthmus of grass. Here a wrought-iron arch supports two 'Mermaid' roses, the clematis *C.* x *jackmanii* and the distinguished evergreen *Clematis armandii* with its leathery leaves and scented waxy flowers in April. In summer the combination of the soft-yellow of the rose and the violet-blue of the *Clematis* x *jackmanii* is extremely effective. Beyond this point the lawn widens out again and there is a work area with a shed and space for a bonfire. At the far end of the garden a large

Josceline Dimbleby's 'clearing in a wood' created by skilful planting.

weeping willow makes a fine hideaway for the children's tree-house.

With limited space the choice of plants has been difficult. Mrs Dimbleby planted two acacias (*Robinia pseudacacia*) when they came to the house in 1972. These are now nearly 30ft high and provide excellent screening. In late June, their blossom is alive with bees and casts its subtle scent over the garden. She decided to retain some pear trees and an elderly box on the west side of the garden. Today, the box is draped with two roses – an enormous *R. filipes* 'Kiftsgate' and one, name unknown, bought by a previous owner in Woolworths for 2/6d. Another 'Kiftsgate', planted in a similar position in the eastern border, covers one of the pear trees; when in flower, these huge roses are like 'two magnificent white waterfalls'. Roses, especially old shrub roses, are among Mrs Dimbleby's favourite plants and she has been influenced in her choice by seeing those at her uncle's garden at Levens Hall in Cumbria. *Rosa gallica versicolor* is her favourite rose and she uses its petals, mixed with others, to make rose-petal ice-cream and jam. She also likes rugosa roses and has planted 'Frau Dagmar Hastrup' and *R. rugosa alba*.

Of the many shrubs planted over the past few years several are now mature specimens. Two *Ceanothus impressus* are now 6ft tall and Mrs Dimbleby finds their association with a *Cotinus coggygria* 'Foliis Purpureis' and an *Elaeagnus* x *ebbingei* very satisfying. At the far end of the garden, near the weeping willow are two of Mrs Dimbleby's favourite plants: a golden philadelphus (*P. coronarius* 'Aureus') to lighten a dark corner and a *Hydrangea sargentiana*, because she loves

Much of the colour in the garden is provided by the variety of flowers on the terrace. They make a perpetually changeable foreground to the luxuriant foliage of the permanent planting behind.

its large velvety leaves. Under the shrubs she has planted cranesbills, particularly *Geranium psilostemon*, and *Anchusa azurea* 'Loddon Royalist', whose sharp blue flowers brighten the darker spaces. A winter-flowering jasmine (*J. nudiflorum*) covers the back of the house with a *Magnolia grandiflora* and the climbing rose, 'New Dawn'. With so much foliage everywhere, the garden looks like a room wall-papered with plants. In fact, Mrs Dimbleby says that it has been her aim to make a garden that resembles 'a clearing in a wood'. She has come to the conclusion that she likes gardens divided into small secluded areas and she intends to divide hers further.

Mrs Dimbleby has always been a keen traveller and has a particular love of India. On her visits there, she has always been impressed by the vibrance of the planting schemes around government buildings and the vast array of plants grown in pots. It was there that she first noticed the variety and sheer exuberance of pansies, which she now counts among her favourite plants. She grows masses of them in pots on the terrace outside the drawing-room windows, mixed with all kinds of other plants in containers: lilies, roses, fuchsias, house-leeks, sweet-peas and tobacco plants. Herb robert and feverfew flourish here.

Mrs Dimbleby says that she does not spend a lot of time gardening; her other commitments simply do not allow it. Much as she loves her town garden she is glad that its manageable size allows her to ignore it on occasion. It is a tribute to her skill that, with so little time, she has been able to make a garden in a small space that is so full of charm and atmosphere.

# Baron Thyssen-Bornemisza in Gloucestershire

**B**ARON THYSSEN SPENDS A GOOD DEAL of his life travelling around the world. Given the choice, he would prefer to spend much more time at his house in Gloucestershire. He was born in the Hague and first came to England in the 1930s to study at Oxford. The outbreak of the war halted his studies but his brief introduction to English life marked the beginning of a love affair with the English countryside. Long before 1978 when he bought his house in the Cotswolds he had decided to make a home in England, but it took time to find the house he wanted.

In Daylesford House he found a fine example of an 18th-century English country house. Designed by S.P.Cockerell and built in Cotswold stone, it is a perfect marriage of elegance and comfort. It was built for Warren Hastings in the 1790s and, somewhat unusually, the park was designed and planting started twenty years before the house was built. The Baron believes that 'Capability' Brown was responsible for its design but no plans survive.

When he bought Daylesford, the Baron was determined to restore house and garden to the state that Cockerell and Brown would have envisaged. Nearly a decade later much has been achieved but, as one might expect of an estate this size, there are always new projects waiting to be undertaken. The Baron says that he is extremely lucky to have a devoted staff of gardeners on whom he can rely to carry out his ideas exactly. The head gardener is Mr Nickless who has worked at Daylesford for 25 years and knows every tree and plant.

The house nestles on the side of a south-facing slope in what seems a very sheltered position. However, this is not the case. According to Mr Nickless, Daylesford has a very exposed garden and nothing remotely tender can be grown unprotected. A long drive passes through delightful undulating Cotswold landscape and sweeps round in an arc to the back of the house. Acres of broadleaf woodland lie behind and the carefully tended park stretches away round three sides of the house. Beyond the park farmland reaches to the horizon with no other buildings visible.

At each corner of the house a grand staircase leads down to a rectangular terrace edged with a balustrade. The Baron calls this his 'only bit of real garden'. It is planted formally with a mixture of HT and Floribunda roses such as 'Mountbatten', 'Korresia', 'Peace' and 'Iceberg'. Prostrate junipers (*Juniperus squamata* 'Blue Carpet') are planted in the corners of the rose beds and in the

The Baron surrounded by the exotic plants which thrive in the unheated orangery.

The lower lake is edged with
moisture-loving plants such as
*Hosta fortunei* 'Marginato-
Alba'.

Facing page

Top: The house and orangery
seen from the other side of the
upper lake. The small island is
planted with slow growing
conifers and prostrate shrubs.

Left: Bedding plants with roses
and dwarf conifers at one end
of the terrace.

Right: The head gardener, Mr
Nickless, with the magnificent
collection of orchids in which
he takes a particular pride.

spring and summer bedding plants add dazzling colour. Cherry trees and variegated hollies have been planted in the beds round the edge of the terrace and rambling rose 'Albertine' twines in and out of the balustrade.

The ground below the terrace falls away sharply to the first of two lakes in the floor of the valley. They were part of the original scheme and are fed from the many springs which rise in the valley. When the Baron came the lakes were clogged with weed and the water was leaking through cracks in their lining. Major engineering work followed in which both lakes were drained, new liners were put in and the banks restored. It took two years for the lakes to refill afterwards but the hard work paid off. Today the water is clear, the banks intact and waterfowl nest on the small islands. The Baron enjoys watching them, saying 'At least the babies have a chance on the islands; the foxes think twice before swimming across.'

The Baron believes that some enormous oaks in the woods are virtually all that remain of the original planting. When he bought the estate, the Baron felt that the woods could be improved, so, with the expert help of the Forestry Commission, a programme of felling and replanting was started. Each year Mr Nickless and his staff also add to the specimen trees and shrubs on the sweeping expanse of grass round the house and lakes. The wide range of trees and their brilliant placing contributes to the breathtaking view over the park from the house. Enormous Scots pines, cedars, chestnuts, oaks, yews and cypresses stand out against the sky on top of the hill to the east of the house. An exceptionally large Leyland cypress (x *Cupressocyparis leylandii*) dominates the slope to the east of the terrace. An evergreen oak (*Quercus ilex*) of great size stands at the top of the first lake, its reflection mirrored in the water. In recent years there have been many additions to the moist area around the top of the first lake. These include a

*Cryptomeria japonica* 'Lobbii' and a deodar (*Cedrus deodara*). At the top of the hill on the east side of the house sorbuses of different kinds have been added to thicken the planting. Here also are some maples, including *Acer negundo* and the purple-leaved sycamore *Acer platanoides* 'Crimson King'. There is a group of magnificent London planes (*Platanus acerifolia*) and the beautiful blue cedar (*Cedrus atlantica glauca*). On the near side of the first lake there is a group of spring flowering-trees – magnolias, amelanchiers and a group of weeping laburnums (*Laburnum anagyroides* 'Pendulum'). Above the second lake, near the house on its west side, there are large specimens of copper beech (*Fagus sylvatica purpurea*) and a cedar of Lebanon (*Cedrus libani*). In front of the copper beech is a young Lawson cypress (*Chamaecyparis lawsoniana* 'Elegantissima'). The drooping sprays of silver-grey foliage are shown off by the darker foliage behind.

Beyond the first lake and to the east of the second, a large wood forms the backdrop for the lakes and screens the kitchen garden which lies on the far side of it. A stream runs through the wood, the water draining from the first lake to flow into the second further down the valley. In a dell just inside the wood, a shrub rose garden was made by the previous owner of the estate, the late Lord Rothermere. This was never very successful however and has gradually been replaced by shrubs propagated from cuttings by Mr Nickless. Today the dell is full of berberises, forsythias, cotoneasters, philadelphuses and hardy fuchsias. From the dell garden a path leads down through the wood following the course of the stream. Over several years this was made into an enormous water garden which now requires almost constant attention to prevent it from becoming choked. Large collections of ferns, astilbes, gunneras, rheums and hostas have been planted along its length and the woodland around has been enriched with large numbers of shrubs to produce a jungle-like density. This is the only part of the garden where rhododendrons and azaleas will thrive and they are planted here in great profusion. There are also many large laurels – the Portugal laurel

Specimen trees are planted on the slopes leading to the lower lake.

(*Prunus lusitanica*) being especially common. Mr Nickless has adopted the habit of planting hydrangeas here after they have been used as pot plants in the house. Here too are lovely lacecap hydrangeas – *H. villosa* and *H. sargentiana*. The climbing hydrangea (*H.petiolaris*) swarms up trees and its flowers hang down over the path.

In another part of the wood is the 'American' walk which leads to the kitchen garden. Here are examples of *Mahonia bealei*, the sweetly scented evergreen *Sarcococca confusa* and the dainty *Philadelphus microphyllus*. A viburnum, *V. plicatum* 'Rowallane', grows beside the path. It is similar to *V. p.* 'Lanarth' but less vigorous. At the end of the walk a gate leads into the two-acre walled kitchen garden. In the previous owner's time, a commercial nursery operated from here, supplying shrubs and trees to other country houses. This has recently been abandoned and now stocks for the estate only are raised. There are extensive greenhouses and a magnificent orchid house.

To the east of the house a path from the courtyard leads to the 18th-century Gothic orangery. It is never heated but its orange and lemon trees bear fruit each season. There are exquisite camellias planted among the fruit trees and large plumbagos (*P. capensis*). On the rear wall there is the pretty white-flowered *Trachelospermum jasminoides* and the beautiful *Brunfelsia pauciflora calcina*, a charming Peruvian plant with large violet flowers that gradually fade to white.

The Baron says that he likes the English country scene very much and the greatest pleasure for him is simply to walk about the grounds at Daylesford. He loves landscape and is much more interested in trees than in flowers although he has always enjoyed visiting other gardens; he has a particular fondness for Sissinghurst. At present his world-wide business interests and the family art gallery in Switzerland take him away from Daylesford far more than he would like. Nowhere else can he find the peace that Daylesford offers and he looks forward to being able to spend more time in this idyllic place.

Left: Roses twine about the balustrade on the terrace. Cockerell's orangery is a particularly delightful feature of the garden.

Right: Dense planting in the woodland garden contrasts sharply with the spacious landscaping elsewhere.

# John Mortimer in Oxfordshire

JOHN MORTIMER BECAME A GARDENER somewhat reluctantly. When his mother died, he inherited the cottage in Oxfordshire which his father had built in 1931. It was the home of his childhood and adolescence, where his father spent long hours creating an immaculate four-acre garden. Mr Mortimer does not know why his father became such a keen gardener. He had never shown any interest in it before he built the cottage. The meticulous diaries in which he recorded the garden's everyday happenings attest to his passion for it and he almost lived his life by its seasons. One entry, for the 28th January 1948, runs: 'Today is mild and sunny. Smith has finished planting the rhododendrons and camellias against the hedge. John was called to the Bar on Jan. 26th.' Even when he became blind his enthusiasm was undiminished. His wife and son became his 'eyes', describing what was happening in the garden and recording it in his diaries. However, John Mortimer was little influenced by this heady horticultural atmosphere. When he took it over he felt totally overwhelmed by the responsibility of such a formidable garden. It had become overgrown but the lingering presence of his father was so intense that he decided that doing nothing was preferable to making mistakes. A rapid return to jungle soon demanded his attention, so that today the garden is very much as it was in his father's time.

The formal garden is entered through an archway cut in a massive cypress screen on the east side of the cottage. From it double-sided borders extend the full length of the garden on this side of the house with a broad grass path running between them. Half-way down, this is crossed at right-angles by another path and where they meet the grass forms a circle. On the north side a path leads past old rhododendrons which need supporting to prevent them from splitting apart. Another path, lying behind the south border, is overshadowed by beech, oak and cedars. The focal point at the far end of the borders is an elegant statue on a plinth flanked by crescent-shaped seats. The whole area between the statue and the house is dominated by the borders. Some of the shrubs were there in Mr Mortimer's father's time but many have been added since his death. The range of shrubs is wide. There are several enormous sweet brooms (*Cytisus multiflora*) with their dazzling white flowers and heavy spring scent, and the semi-prostrate broom (*C.* x *kewensis*) with masses of creamy-yellow flowers in May. Cotoneasters and virburnums are found in variety and several snowy mespiluses (*Amelanchier lamarckii*) with their delicate white spring flowers and rich red-bronze foliage in the autumn. Mount Etna broom (*Genista aetnensis*) thrives in the borders, as does the bridal wreath (*Spiraea* x *arguta*). There is a magnificent beauty bush (*Kolkwitzia amabilis*) hung with soft pink bell-shaped flowers in

John Mortimer at the far end of the double borders made by his father.

June. Evergreens include mahonias, berberises, escallonias and *Osmanthus delavayi* with its small leathery leaves and fragrant flowers in April. There are buddleias, deutzias and weigelas which punctuate the borders at regular intervals. Mr Mortimer has also added different kinds of pieris. Their flower panicles are formed in the autumn and open the following spring. Some have red-tinged buds which are attractive throughout the winter. One of the best is *P. formosa* var. *forrestii* with its red young shoots and large, scented flowers. On the edge of the path beneath the trees are some Japanese maples – particularly members of the 'Dissectum' group. Climbing roses are being trained up pillars on the corner of each border and actinidias (*Actinidia kolomikta*) grow up stakes within the borders.

Among the shrubs in the borders there is a generous mixture of hardy perennials. Traditional cottage-garden plants like lupins and cranesbills are found as well as hostas, hellebores and astilbes. More unusual plants include the foxtail lily (*Eremurus bungei*) with long golden spikes of flowers and the blue Himalayan poppy (*Meconopsis baileyi*) with its delicate sky-blue flowers thriving in the shade. Another shade-loving plant that is well represented is goat's beard (*Aruncus sylvester*) with plumes like pampas grass and ferny leaves.

Mr Mortimer's father planted the yew trees behind the statue to screen the shrub borders from the woodland planting beyond. From the statue a shady path leads into the orchard. The entrance to it is marked by an ancient unidentified viburnum of immense size makes a dramatic sight in June with its white blossom. Old apple trees are mixed with ornamental cherries. There is a large specimen of the cherry 'Shimidsu Zakura' with its flattened crown rather like an umbrella and pure white flowers which hang all along the branches in clusters. An old and gnarled specimen of the thorn *Crataegus crus-galli* has spread into a bulbous shape which Mr Mortimer says reminds him of a Japanese wrestler. An enormous eucryphia (*E. cordifolia*) was planted by Mr Mortimer and his father

Part of the long borders in early summer. *Cytisus* x *kewensis* contrasts with *Viburnum davidii* behind facing *Kerria japonica* 'Pleniflora' and a brilliant red azalea.

the day he met his wife Penelope. Several whitebeams have grown very large and form a canopy over the path at the far end of the orchard. There is a beautiful specimen of the Persian iron tree (*Parrotia persica*) whose leaves turn a glorious crimson in the autumn. Recent additions include a maidenhair tree (*Ginkgo biloba*), a corkscrew hazel (*Corylus avellana* 'Contorta') a blue cedar (*Cedrus atlantica glauca*) and a Japanese pagoda tree (*Sophora japonica*) which in due course will be festooned with white pea-like flowers in late summer and autumn.

On the south side of the house, a paved terrace is edged with borders of bush roses and a *Hydrangea petiolaris* grows on the wall. Below the terrace a gently sloping lawn has as its only ornament a graceful tulip tree (*Liriodendron tulipifera*) which flowers every four or five years. A hedge separates the house and lawn from the productive kitchen garden. On its lawn side wide beds are planted with early flowering rhododendrons and daphnes (*D. mezereum*). They are underplanted with elephants' ears (bergenia hybrids) and spring bulbs. The kitchen garden is an important element of the garden for Mr Mortimer. His ideal would be a cottage garden with vegetables and flowers mixed together.

Having begun as a reluctant gardener, Mr Mortimer undoubtedly now finds the garden plays an important part in his life. He dislikes London, going there as seldom as possible, preferring to write in the tranquillity of his study at the cottage. He would love to write in the garden but he finds it too distracting; he needs the discipline of a set working pattern, tucked away out of sight. Although he enjoys travelling abroad, he would not want to live anywhere other than England, saying, 'It is difficult to write away from the sound of one's own language.' He says he never would have become a lawyer, certainly not a gardener, without his father's influence but the days when his father's presence dominated the garden are over. By adding plants and ideas of his own while retaining the framework of the garden Mr Mortimer has achieved a happy balance between the past and the present.

# Prue Leith in Gloucestershire

*I*T MAY BE THAT similar gifts are revealed in those who have mastered the arts of cookery and of gardening. Both need imagination, good organisation and an artistic eye. Prue Leith became a professional cook long before she became a gardener and has found the discipline of the kitchen a great help in her gardening. And she brings to her gardening the same kind of enthusiasm and dedication that has made her name in the cookery world.

She still regards herself as a novice in horticultural matters. Before she and her husband bought their farm in the Cotswolds in the mid-1970s, she had never had a garden and never wanted one. A succession of intimidating gardeners who knew exactly what should be done and when, left Miss Leith feeling that, as a breed, chefs were much easier to deal with. It was only when she acquired her present gardener, Ray Pearse, whom she describes as an enthusiastic amateur like herself, that she felt she could contribute something to the garden. Now she says they learn together, experimenting all the time and labelling meticulously in case they forget what things are. There was a time when they ordered plants which turned out to be things they already had. Ray now keeps strict records so mistakes are becoming rarer.

A farm in Gloucestershire, with cattle churning muddy paths across the fields that surround the garden, is a far cry from Miss Leith's childhood home in Johannesburg where her parents had a large garden. Today, however, she has no desire to grow the exotic native plants of South Africa which she feels are unsuited to the English landscape. Her aim is to achieve what she calls 'the English look; casual and floppy and with so much in a bed that no bare earth can be seen'.

Her garden has what she calls 'enviable bones'. It was laid out in Victorian times and covers five acres. The mature trees, and hedges of yew and beech, provide the setting for all the new planting of the past four years.

Miss Leith still finds that her tastes are constantly changing as she visits other gardens. However, she loves shrub roses and has planted dozens in recent years. They are everywhere: beside the drive, around the croquet lawn, in the courtyard, growing up the house, climbing over the pergola in the sunken garden and edging the large lawn. Pink and white are the chief colours along the drive. Here Miss Leith grows one of her favourites, the Damask rose 'Madame Hardy' with great double white flowers and a delicious scent with a hint of lemon in it. Nearby is a group of hybrid musk roses – 'Penelope', 'Cornelia' and 'Francesca'. There is also the magnificent old Alba rose 'Celestial' with its semi-double pink flowers and exquisite heavy scent. When she noticed that

On the south side of the house soft colours envelope the terrace.

many of the shrub roses were flopping over and growing towards the light, she designed simple metal supports and had them made by a local blacksmith. Now the roses are well supported and the supports are almost invisible.

On one side of the drive, the roses have a background of old evergreen oaks (*Quercus ilex*), larch and laurels; on the other side, there is a long beech hedge which forms one side of the kitchen garden. West of the drive, towards the house, there is a croquet lawn. Miss Leith and her husband have added new trees, shrubs and roses to the area between the drive and the croquet lawn, skilfully mixing light and dark foliage. A golden Indian bean tree (*Catalpa bignonioides* 'Aurea') has been planted next to a Japanese maple, *Acer palmatum* 'Heptalobum Osakazuki', which has brilliant autumn colour, and a birch with exceptionally white bark, *Betula jacquemontii*. They have also planted a weeping silver lime (*Tilia petiolaris*) and a golden-leaved form of the western red cedar (*Thuja plicata* 'Aurea'). Nearby are more roses – *R. glauca*, the valuable white-flowered hybrid perpetual 'Frau Karl Druschki' and the Bourbon 'Boule de Neige'. A group of *Rosa* 'Nevada' flanks a golden-leaved robinia (*R. pseudacacia* 'Frisia') on the far side of the croquet lawn.

A wide terrace runs along the south and west sides of the house, surrounded by a low stone wall. The gaps in the paving on the terrace and in the top of the wall contain all kinds of alpine and low-growing plants. There are many different thymes, dwarf campanulas, houseleeks, rockery phloxes and pinks crammed into every crack and crevice.

Outside the drawing-room windows, to the south of the croquet lawn, a statue of a boy stands in the middle of a lawn. Nearby, parallel yew hedges back double herbaceous borders planted in blue, yellow and white. Among traditional perennials like campanulas, delphiniums, white lupins, echinops, hostas, lady's mantle and the roses 'Buff Beauty', 'Frühlingsgold' and 'Iceberg', the newer additions include *Sisyrinchium striatum*, *Geranium renardii*, *Stokesia laevis*, *Caryopteris* x *clandonensis*, the prostrate evening primrose, *Oenothera missouriensis*, *Iris foetidissima* 'Variegata', the intensely blue-flowered *Ceratostigma plumbaginoides*, the feathery *Artemisia glacialis* and the yellow urn-shaped flowers of *Allium flavum*. One of Miss Leith's favourite jobs is clearing these beds in the

Left: The elegant outlines of cordylines in pots contrast with the bold planting of the red garden below.

Right: Prue Leith and her chinese-red pavilion on the lake's island with the house in the background.

Blue, yellow and white predominate in this mixed border where perennials associate happily with roses.

autumn when the frosts come. At their far end, the focal point is a statue of a man sitting deep in thought. He was rescued from Stratford where he had been a prop in the play *The Odd Couple*. He is made of fibre-glass but Miss Leith has painted him to look exactly like bronze. Beyond the yew hedges there is a fine group of Scots pine, ash, sycamore, beech and a handsome blue spruce (*Picea pungens* 'Glauca'). These trees are underplanted with philadelphus, *Viburnum plicatum* 'Lanarth' and the lovely golden elder (*Sambucus racemosa* 'Plumosa Aurea') with its creamy flower panicles.

The largest lawn in the garden, on the south side of the house, has been kept free of any planting, so as not to detract from the view of the countryside beyond. However Miss Leith has planted a hedge of the striped rose *R. gallica versicolor* directly below the terrace. Several years ago she and her husband decided to excavate a lake in one of the fields beyond this south lawn. Drainage has always been a problem there and they thought a lake would enhance the view from the house. The excavation was not without problems but eventually they got their lake with its own small island. A Chinoiserie bridge was added and a pagoda-shaped pavilion placed on the island. Miss Leith saw the pavilion at the Chelsea Flower Show and bought it on impulse. They decided to paint both the bridge and the pavilion bright red – a daring choice for the Gloucestershire countryside which nevertheless succeeds. Now they are planting up the area

round the lake – a project involving a lot of hard work as the soil is heavy clay. Large amounts of compost and leaf-mould are incorporated into the planting holes. Willows, dogwoods and the snowy mespilus (*Amelanchier canadensis*) have been planted and a start is being made on perennials.

To the east of the house, near the kitchen, there is a small sunken garden with a pergola and all the beds surrounding this area have been planted with red-flowered plants. Miss Leith says that she did it 'to cock a snook at all my posh gardening friends who don't hold with such vulgar displays of colour', but, surprisingly, has found that the effect is not half so jarring as she had expected and that the beds provide welcome colour late in the season. She grows a wide variety of plants here. Red tobacco plants, petunias, salvias and pansies are mixed with perennials such as *Sidalcea* 'Croftway Red', *Lobelia cardinalis*, *Sedum hidalcanum*, *Sedum maximum atropurpureum*, *Zauschneria californica* – the Californian fuchsia – and *Iris chrysographes*. The roses 'Parkdirektor Riggers' and 'Josephine Bruce' grow up the pergola and there are bushes of the velvety red floribunda 'Evelyn Fison' in the beds.

The walls of the house provide the home for a *Magnolia grandiflora*, the rose 'New Dawn' and more tender plants like *Solanum crispum* with its soft blue flowers and a passion flower (*Passiflora caerulea*). In the beds at their feet the emphasis is on soft colours – grey plants, white petunias, pale deutzias and variegated dogwoods.

Although she admits to being very neat herself, Miss Leith says that her husband is even more concerned about the tidiness of the garden. He loves immaculate grass and has started to remove the moss from all the lawns. Ideally,

From the terrace there are views of the lovely Cotswold landscape. Masses of alpines grow among the paving stones and on top of the walls.

Left: One end of the herbaceous borders looking west.

Right: The kitchen garden has recently been transformed into a French-style *jardin potager*.

Miss Leith would like to see all the hedges underplanted with groundcover plants like wood-ruff and *Tiarella cordifolia* but her husband disagrees. As a matter of principle she grows only those plants that will thrive in her garden with no special attention as she cannot see the point in struggling with tender species only to see them carried off by a severe winter – 'I have enough problems growing easy things.'

Her pride and joy is the kitchen garden. She changed this into a French-style *jardin potager* two years ago, based on the famous one at Villandry and on her friend Robert Carrier's garden. Here she grows vegetables and the all-important herbs for her cookery school and restaurant. Alongside the *potager*, there is a newly planted orchard with a wide variety of apples, plums and pears. It is one of Miss Leith's greatest pleasures to walk round the *potager* in the spring and admire its finely-tilled earth and neat rows of young plants. She says that its regimented neatness gives her 'the same satisfaction as seeing a clean surface in a kitchen'.

In her earliest gardening days, Miss Leith says that she was wildly impulsive and insisted on planting all kinds of plants without sufficient preparation of the soil, but she has learnt from her mistakes and new areas are rigorously prepared before planting. She thinks that the worlds of cooking and of gardening have much in common. Gardeners appear to be just as generous about swapping plants and ideas as cooks are with their recipes. Looking forward to the time when she can do more gardening than cooking, Miss Leith says, 'Ideally, I would like to retire and be a gardener.' At present it seems that she has mastered both arts with equal success.

# The Hon. Alan Clark in Kent

SALTWOOD CASTLE IS TODAY more a private family home than it has ever been in its long history. The Hon. Alan Clark and his wife moved into the castle when Mr Clark's father, the art historian Lord Clark, moved to a new house he had built in the grounds in 1972. Mr Clark has always loved Saltwood passionately and, with his wife, has maintained it with a deep feeling for its history and atmosphere. Although Mrs Clark claims that she and her husband are 'complete failures as gardeners', their ideals of conservation and continuity suit the setting perfectly.

Mr Clark's mother created much of the structure of the garden. She adored the daffodils, which today surround the castle in spring and she was also responsible for planting many of the roses. The character of the garden is romantic and wild. The great castle walls and picturesque ruins are such a dominating backdrop that tamed and precise borders would seem quite unsuitable. As it is the Clarks love plants of all sorts to seed themselves wherever they will with minimum interference. They also actively encourage wildlife and 'rush around opening windows' so that swallows can swoop about the vaulted ceilings.

Inside the great curtain walls of the castle there is a vast expanse of grass. Mr Clark enjoys mowing this lawn, finds the four hours which the job takes relaxing, and never tires of 'watching the marvellous shadows'. On the south side of the lawn lie the remains of the early 14th-century hall. It is roofless but preserves fine tracery windows. Its floor is carpeted with moon daisies and feverfew and a hop is being trained up one wall. One of the windows is framed by the handsome Edwardian rose 'Paul's Lemon Pillar'. At the west end of the hall a small lawn, edged with seedling yews, is backed by white buddleias (*B. fallowiana alba*). Next to this is the rose garden with many old varieties surrounded by box hedging and the highly scented American rambler 'Francis E. Lester'.

A gap in the wall behind the rose garden leads to the Secret Garden. In the 1380s this was Archbishop Courtenay's private enclave – the only entrance to it leading from his private apartments. Two enormous bays flank the doorway and white buddleias are planted in the quartered grass squares.

In the north-west corner of the main garden an old and rampant herbaceous border curls round the castle wall. Here self-sown additions jostle with plants of nobler ancestry. It is an emphatic piece of planting with roses, lilies, delphiniums, bear's breeches (*Acanthus mollis*), Jacob's ladder (*Polemonium caeruleum*), hollyhocks and the great 'Kiftsgate' rose (*R. filipes* 'Kiftsgate') scaling the wall behind. 'I should chuck out the anchusa but the bees love it,' says Mrs Clark and adds, slightly despairingly, 'We throw the compost heap over the beds but all

The Hon. Alan and Mrs Clark
framed in a window of the
Great Hall.

73

one feeds is the bindweed.' The Clarks are very strongly against the use of chemicals in the garden.

East of the herbaceous border clumps of pampas grass (*Cortaderia selloana*) shelter an ornamental swimming pool. Below the walls foliage plants and climbers thrive. This exotic corner is further embellished by a pair of Attic columns from the island of Delos.

At various points around the walls, stairways circle up dark turrets and give access to the ramparts. The Clarks think of their garden as 'everywhere it can grow' and this includes the ramparts. Red, pink and white valerian grows from the cracks, house-leeks and toadflax fringe the parapet. Until recently the gardener had to haul up the mower to trim the grass path but he now uses a more manageable strimmer to do the job. The Clarks occasionally have to remove tree saplings from the castle walls – 'with the slight risk that the walls might fall down'. The Russian vine (*Polygonum baldschuanicum*) reaches up to the highest tower and drapes the walls with its greenish-white panicles. Rambling roses peep over the top and scent the walk round the parapet. Peacocks bask in the warmest spots up here. Mrs Clark resigns herself to the fact that 'anything peacock height gets eaten'.The ramparts overlook a pond which has been excavated by the Clarks where part of the moat would have been. It is filled with terrapins, goldfish, tench, carp and orfe – much to the delight of the visiting herons.

Outside the southern wall are the upper and lower terraces where two borders,

Top: The garden seen from the vantage point of the ramparts.

Left: Half-hidden doorways lead to the ramparts' stairways. Self-sown plants and cascading roses fill this sheltered corner.

Right: The rose garden created by Mr Clark's mother where the old roses are hedged with box.

one above the other, are informally planted with perennials and annuals such as Shasta daisies and Canterbury bells (*Campanula medium*) and many shrub roses. Sadly, a fine collection of cistuses, planted by Mr Clark's mother, was decimated in the winter of 1985/6. Above these borders the high walls are festooned with rambling roses – 'Albertine', 'Albéric Barbier', 'Emily Gray' and *Rosa banksiae lutea*.

A path leads through a small orchard which is a mass of daffodils and primroses in spring and cow parsley in early summer. Here the grass is left uncut until autumn. In a corner on the south side of the gatehouse there is an effective planting of the Mexican orange (*Choisya ternata*), with its fragrant shiny dark-green foliage, and the climbing rose 'Wedding Day'. This rose has produced 'sports' with an attractive double flower. Below the gatehouse the Clarks have planted a mulberry and near it is a tulip tree (*Liriodendron tulipifera*) planted by the Queen Mother in 1957.

Mr Clark treasures his weekends at Saltwood – 'the most wonderful place in the world'. In order to maintain the castle in the way he believes to be best, he refuses to take any public money for its upkeep. Just as Saltwood Castle remains free of the rather institutional stamp that marks many other historic buildings – so too does the garden. Mr Clark, who believes that a true appreciation of gardening comes only in middle-age, wants 'to do things that my grand-children will thank me for'. His sympathetic care for their inheritance has assured that castle and garden now make an extremely individual but harmonious whole.

# David Hicks in Oxfordshire

DAVID HICKS THINKS THAT everyone should have 'nostalgic' plants in their gardens which can conjure up both happy and sad memories. Two tubs of rhododendrons (which he dislikes) serve to remind him of the 'rhododendron country' round his Sussex prep school. However, their purpose is not to remind him of the unfailing misery of his schooldays but to emphasise how happy and fulfilled his life has been since.

Gardens and gardening always seem to have played a part in his life. Inspired by parents who were both keen gardeners, he made his first garden when he was six, sowing annual seeds bought at Woolworths. Mr Hicks's interest in gardening may well come from his parents, but his ideas about gardens have been formulated over many years through visiting others and surveying them with his keen designer's eye. Today, the ones that he most admires are those with what he calls 'a strong sense of style', quoting as an example the Duchess of Beaufort's former garden at the Dower House, Badminton: 'The best garden made in England since the war.' As an interior decorator, he confesses to preferring those that resemble the layout of buildings; gardens made of rooms with vistas and glimpses into other rooms – 'architectural gardening' is how he describes it. He has no desire to create a garden full of rare and exotic plants. He says he is not a plantsman but feels that he has sufficient knowledge to decide which plants he wants in his own garden and which he does not. In any case he is firmly convinced that women are far greater connoisseurs of plants than men are. To him the perfect garden must have a strong formal element; he loves the idea of 'space punctuated by lines', an approach to gardening that owes much to the classical ideal. It might sound as if his gardening conforms to rigidly predetermined rules; it does not. He makes his rules and then breaks them with vigour and originality.

He began work on his present garden in 1980 when he and Lady Pamela bought the farmhouse at Brightwell Baldwin. When they first saw it there was no garden to speak of; the house had been at the heart of a working farm and the barns, dairy and farmyard backed right up to it. They found brick and stone walls between the buildings which divided the yard into enclosures: the perfect place to make an architectural garden. These decorative structures now contribute enormously to the garden's character.

Before any work started, Mr Hicks mapped it all out carefully on graph paper, deciding that he must have vistas from both drawing-room and dining-room and doorways between the various enclosures. A digger was brought in 'to get the levels right', to excavate a pool outside the dining-room and to make a raised

Chestnut hedges flank the pool.
Behind is the 'Mediterranean'
pot garden.

terrace on the south side of the dining-room enclosure. He decided to leave the area in front of the house largely untouched. The long drive to the house needed some replacement trees, but the meadow in front of it was perfect. A huge old ilex (*Quercus ilex*) stands at its centre and in spring the whole meadow is swamped with masses of daffodils and snake's head fritillaries (*Fritillaria meleagris*). Beyond it, farmland stretches away as far as the eye can see. He chose to keep the front of the house as simple as possible – its pretty 18th-century facade needing little embellishment. Two Versailles tubs were placed at the front corners of the house and planted with bay trees; sadly these succumbed after a very cold winter and have been replaced with standard hawthorns which will be clipped into ball shapes in time. Outside the front door, on either side of a pretty tracery porch, he has placed pots of gooseberries, which are being clipped into balls. Nearby, growing up the front of the house, are the climbing roses 'Lady Waterlow' and 'Gloire de Dijon'.

Although the brick and stone walls were a bonus, they did block the view of the surrounding farmland from the back of the house. Mr Hicks decided to cut out sections of them opposite the drawing-room and dining-room windows to produce the long views he wanted. To frame the vista from the drawing-room, he planted parallel lines of hornbeams – standards and hedges, with a wide space between the lines. At the far end of these lines, he made a *clairvoyée* in the new gap in the wall. Through this the farmland can be glimpsed in the distance. At the house end of the hornbeams, and at right angles to them, he planted another two lines, to create L-shapes, and put a small recess in the angle of each L to house 18th-century stone urns on plinths. Behind the eastern L of hornbeams he planted a block of trees and shrubs. Trees such as oaks, chestnuts and whitebeams stand alongside buddleias, philadelphuses, viburnums, hawthorns, hydrangeas, a tulip tree (*Liriodendron tulipifera*), golden elders (*Sambucus racemosa* 'Plumosa Aurea') and Indian bean trees (*Catalpa bignonioides*). In the western L there is a single slab of lime hedging.

The drawing-room garden is the largest walled area of the garden, so there is space on either side of the hornbeams and in front of them near the house. A well-tended lawn lies between the house and trees – 'all Regency stripes', says

Facing page

Top: The 'family' rose border in early summer. Before the roses are in flower this border overflows with subtle shades and textures of green and yellow foliage.

Left: David Hicks glimpsed through one of the many stylish doorways that are such a feature of his garden,

Right: On the terrace outside the dining room, small beds contain plants of contrasting foliage.

The unusual American poke weed (*Phytolacca americana*) seeds itself about the garden. Here it is effectively fringed with flowering chives.

Mr Hicks. At one side of it, a classical marble statue stands on a plinth. This is the cause of a mild disagreement between Mr Hicks and his son. It is covered in lichen which Mr Hicks likes; his son would like to clean it. Mr Hicks says, smiling, that he suspects that as soon as he is dead his son will be 'out there with a scrubbing brush and bleach'.

To the east of the hornbeams there is a square of grass, and in the centre stands a young *Magnolia grandiflora* 'Exmouth'. Mr Hicks hopes to grow it as a free-standing specimen, so for the moment it is surrounded by a wooden shelter to protect it from the cold wind. Around the edge of the grass is the recent addition of a pergola which runs along three sides of the square. This is being covered with climbing plants of all kinds to make a tapestry tunnel. Climbing roses like 'New Dawn', 'Schoolgirl' and the climbing form of 'Iceberg' are intermingled with clematises 'The President', 'Hagley Hybrid' and 'Nellie Moser' and honeysuckles: *Lonicera japonica flexuosa* with red to purple buds and red stems, and both *L. periclymenum* 'Belgica' and 'Serotina'. There is also the more unusual Dutchman's pipe (*Aristolochia macrophylla*), a vigorous deciduous climber which has yellow, brown and green flowers.

To the west of the hornbeams and the block of lime hedging lie the herbaceous borders which run parallel to the main lines of trees. The borders have strongly defined castellated edges and a wide grass path runs between them. The planting has been restricted to soft colours – white, pink, blue and mauve with a hint of yellow. Within this controlled colour-scheme there are plants of boldly contrasting shapes and sizes; all have been chosen with the utmost care, not only for their individual merit but also for their contribution to the overall picture. At the height of the season the effect is one of airy exuberance. All the plants are repeated at regular intervals down the borders and the close planting ensures that there are no gaps. At the back, there are espalier-trained 'Albertine' roses and clumps of the beautiful *Crambe cordifolia*. Towards the front standard 'Nozomi' roses are surrounded with the delicate hydrangea 'Madame E. Mouillère' and the American poke weed (*Phytolacca americana*) with its hydrangea-like leaves and erect white flower spikes which are followed by maroon berries. There are lots of lilies (*L. auratum* and *L. regale*), stately against

Left: The front door is flanked with standard gooseberries which will be clipped into ball shapes.

Right; The 'secret' rose garden – made from an old piggery.

Facing page

The long pergola covered in the rambling rose 'American Pillar'.

80

Facing page

Top: Looking towards the dining-room window which overlooks the pool.

Bottom: The long vista from the dining-room window to the gap made by Mr Hicks in the woods on the horizon.

the feathery bracts of *Salvia turkestanica* and the handsome *Hosta sieboldii*. Sedums provide colour later in the season and scent comes from a variety of pinks but principally from the frilly-edged white 'Mrs Sinkins', one of Mr Hicks's favourites.

At the house end of the borders, and facing them, there is a bed where Mr Hicks grows what he calls 'family roses'. The pale yellow 'Mountbatten', 'Margaret von Hessen' and 'Lady Romsey' grow near trellis-work pyramids which are smothered in honeysuckle and 'Constance Spry' roses. At each corner there is the tree-paeony *Paeonia lutea* 'Ludlowii' and artichokes to provide startling contrasts of leaf form. Lady's mantle fills in the spaces between the roses and spills over onto the grass. Around the corner, near the house, one of Mr Hicks's gothic doorways leads to the dining-room garden. On either side of it there are beds where Mr Hicks grows his favourite hosta *H. sieboldii* with verbascums and *Acanthus spinosus*. These provide a wonderfully architectural foreground for the white flowers of the clematises 'Henryi' and 'Miss Bateman' growing up the wall behind. Outside the drawing-room windows there are small rectangular beds full of bergenias brought by Mr Hicks from his previous house. Next to them there is a narrow terrace where he has put some Chippendale-style seats of his own design.

A door in the wall at the far end of the herbaceous borders leads to another area of the garden where there is a long border and small beds full of roses for cutting. From here another door opens into what is possibly Mr Hicks's favourite place: the rose garden. This secret garden has been made in the rectangular walled area that used to be the piggery and, as Mr Hicks feels that one should have to retrace one's steps from a secret garden, it has only one entrance. This is a beautiful small garden where the roses have been given full rein to grow as they

The 'Regency stripes' of the lawn lead the eye to the *clairvoyée* in the wall of the drawing-room garden.

The herbaceous borders with castellated edges in high summer. The plants have been carefully chosen both for their own merit as well as for their contribution to the total effect.

will, with the result that the space appears to be filled with a three-dimensional tapestry of white, pink, mauve, red and purple. The roses flop over the path and provide an exquisite frame for a stone urn on a plinth which is the focal point at the far end of the central path. They are mostly old shrub roses like 'Fantin Latour', 'Pierre Oger', the rugosas 'Blanc Double de Coubert' and 'Roseraie de l'Hay', with climbers like 'Bobbie James', 'New Dawn' and 'Félicité et Perpétue'. Honeysuckles twine among the roses and clumps of chives are used ornamentally to fringe the paths.

Entering the dining-room garden through the gothic door from the drawing-room garden, the first feature to catch the eye is a raised cobbled terrace on the south side of the door. A flint alcove in the centre of the wall contains a bronze relief of Lady Mountbatten, Lady Pamela's mother, and Mr Hicks has put Lutyens seats at either end of the terrace and a collection of terracotta pots among the cobbles. In spring they are crammed with tulips, providing a vibrant splash of colour to what is otherwise a largely green garden. Later in the summer, lilies, pelargoniums and hostas with bushes of lavender planted in spaces in the cobbles give a Mediterranean quality. A slight slope leads from the terrace to the area around the black-painted pool. Mr Hicks decided to plant lines of Indian chestnuts (*Aesculus indica*) down the long sides of the pool with chestnut hedges below them. When he ordered the hedging the nurseryman told him that he could not have it as chestnut was unsuitable for a hedge. Mr Hicks insisted and the hedges are growing well in their allotted position. From the pool, the lines of chestnuts lead the eye to the farmland beyond the garden and to a stand of trees on the horizon in which Mr Hicks has cut a gap which precisely aligns with the pool.

Beyond the barns on the north side of the dining-room garden, the old horse pond is the site of some dramatic water-side plants. Here is the massive giant hogweed (*Heracleum mantegazzianum*) near the arum lily (*Zantedeschia aethiopica*) with its white spathes and arrow-like leaves, and *Peltiphyllum peltatum*, a perennial with large round leaves and pink flowers. Near the pond are some flowering cherries, put here so that they cannot be seen from the house as Mr Hicks considers their blossom too garish to fit in with his planting schemes. He grows them simply to provide blossom for the house; an idea he discovered in Japan where it is common to cut off the whole crown of a small tree to provide a spectacular decoration in a house or hotel. The trees recover very quickly from this apparently savage treatment and within a couple of years are ready for a further decapitation.

Another area behind the house contains a small paddock where lines of lime trees lead to the tennis court. The tennis court is screened by a long rustic pergola covered with 'American Pillar' roses, another of Mr Hicks's 'nostalgic' plants. When he was young it seemed that every garden he went to was filled with it, and although he dislikes it he had to have it in his own.

At all stages in the planning and planting of his garden Mr Hicks has been actively involved and can often be found working alongside Steve Magden, his gardener for the past 21 years. A long and close association with plants has given Mr Hicks strong likes and dislikes. His pet hates are Leyland cypresses, forsythia bushes (although they may be acceptable as a hedge), silver birches, fastigiate trees like *Prunus* 'Amanagowa' and plants with variegated leaves – 'they look diseased'. The plants he especially likes are all old shrub roses, the rose 'Constance Spry', 'Nozomi' roses trained as standards, Rembrandt tulips and practically all trees. It depresses him that three-quarters of all the trees supplied to local authorities by his favourite nurserymen, Notcutts of Suffolk, are destroyed by vandals. However, he regrets that he did not have the courage to take down all the trees in his garden and start again; 'I could not bear to do it.'

Mr Hicks is very firmly of the opinion that 'Capability' Brown and Repton were the worst influences on English gardening and have much to answer for, destroying, as they did, many lovely Elizabethan and 17th-century gardens to create their own idealised landscape. His own garden has been planned with an eye for the future and he does not expect to see it to maturity. He hopes his sons, and grandsons, will benefit from his judicious planting. 'Having a garden is like having another family,' he says, 'It needs to be constantly cared for, but without too much fuss.'

A bronze relief of Lady Mountbatten set in a flint alcove.

# Evelyn Anthony in Essex

T HE NOVELIST EVELYN ANTHONY (Mrs Michael Ward-Thomas) describes her first attempts at gardening as 'growing mud'. She learnt the rudiments of it in Hertfordshire when she and her husband moved from London to a cottage in 1957. As a child and the daughter of a naval officer peripatetic existence meant that there was never enough time in one place for gardening. In Hertfordshire, with six young children, and her writing occupying so much of her time, she could not pursue her new hobby as much as she would have liked. It was when they moved to Horham Hall, a fine pre-Reformation house, that she really became a gardener. Here the six-acre garden was in an immaculate condition and Mrs Ward-Thomas vividly remembers the panic and awe it inspired in her. In those days neither she, her husband nor their gardener knew enough; so they learnt together, making what she now calls 'some ghastly mistakes'.

Horham is dominated by intricate Tudor brickwork. The bricks would have been made on site and a small pond beside the drive is probably the flooded clay pit from which they were made. Apart from the house itself they were used to build several enclosures nearby. The largest of these lies to the west of the drive and contains a circular lake. This is reached from the house by way of a paved terrace and a large lawn. Around the lake groups of trees stand in rough grass which in spring is clothed in drifts of daffodils. Sadly, all the elms have been lost and Mrs Ward-Thomas is relieved that she planted some cypresses on the edge of the lake garden 20 years ago. Now they are the only barrier between the garden and the farmland beyond, helping to protect it from the ravages of the cold Essex winter winds. Beside the lake, among the willows, a maidenhair tree (*Ginkgo biloba*) planted some years ago continues to grow at an alarming rate so Mr Ward-Thomas prunes it from time to time. On one bank he has planted viburnums (*V. plicatum* 'Lanarth') which will in time replace others that are showing their age. Nearby a group of cotoneasters (*C.* x *watereri* 'John Waterer') have grown inwards forming a mushroom shape. In spring the ground beneath is carpeted with *Anemone blanda*.

A magnificent old brick wall provides the backdrop for Mrs Ward-Thomas's herbaceous border on the east side of the lake garden. Three small recesses in it were the falcons' 'stops' or mews where they were kept when not out hunting. Mrs Ward-Thomas has added an Italian marble plaque as her own embellishment to the garden and 'to leave something permanent behind'. She has filled the border with favourite plants, both shrubs and brightly coloured perennials. There are several bleeding hearts (*Dicentra spectabilis*), a ligularia (*L. dentata*

Mr and Mrs Ward-Thomas
sitting in spring sunshine by
the falcons' mews.

'Desdemona') which threatens to swamp the border so has to be divided regularly; paeonies, lilies, delphiniums, pinks, astilbes, potentillas and, for colour later in the season, michaelmas daisies. Three golden elders (*Sambucus racemosa* 'Plumosa Aurea') make a fine feature in the border. It is a favourite plant and, with its bright golden leaves, one of the most striking foliage shrubs.

Across the lawn near the terrace, in complete contrast, is a small sheltered white and silver bed. At its centre a weeping pear (*Pyrus salicifolia* 'Pendula') is kept trimmed. In spring it is surrounded by pure white daffodils ('A.P.Milner'). Iceberg roses and lilacs ('Madame Lemoine' and 'Monique Lemoine', both with double flowers, and 'Maud Notcutt', single flowers – all cultivars of *Syringa vulgaris*) are underplanted with lambs' ears (*Stachys lanata* and its cultivar 'Silver Carpet' – a more compact form which does not flower). There are clumps of artemisias (*A.* 'Powis Castle' and *A. nutans* 'Silver Queen') and Solomon's seal. A rampant white clematis was removed as it was obscuring the design of the brickwork behind.

On the western side of the lake a large shrub border screens the tennis court from the lake garden. Its collection of deutzias and philadelphuses has been added to with smoke bushes (*Cotinus coggygria* and its form 'Royal Purple') and dogwoods (*Cornus alba* 'Elegantissima' and *C.a.* 'Spaethii').

Between the white and silver border and the shrub border an opening leads to a long walk. It is bounded on its north side by a wall of the old vegetable garden. A sunny border runs along its length. Part of it is another special province of Mrs Ward-Thomas. At Hidcote she saw a mixed planting of hydrangeas and was so impressed that she has started to adopt the idea herself. She plans to mix the hydrangeas with other shrubs – 'Anything that will be easy to manage when I can't get down to the weeding,' she says. At present the bed is filled with Lenten roses (*Helleborus orientalis* hybrids) lilies, hostas, paeonies, tulips, and *Brunnera macrophylla*, the evergreen *Skimmia japonica*, several buddleias (forms of *B.*

Drifts of daffodils border the drive in spring. The pair of stone urns mark the entrance to the courtyard on the eastern side of the house.

Left: Clipped box shapes at the entrance to Mrs Ward-Thomas's hydrangea border. Their architectural shape is in keeping with the assortment of gables, spires and turrets of the Tudor house.

Right: An ingenious raft on the lake provides a sanctuary for the ducks protecting them from foxes. It can be drawn to the bank on pulleys.

*davidii*) and climbing roses. Further along the wall Mr Ward-Thomas has planted up a bed with rugosa roses, using two of his favourites – 'Blanc Double de Coubert' and 'Roseraie de l'Hay'. They are interspersed with ornamental chaenomeles (*C.* x *superba* 'Knap Hill Scarlet'), hollies and Jews' mallow (*Kerria japonica* 'Pleniflora'). A new feature are paired beds on the edge of the tennis court planted with Mr Ward-Thomas's varied collection of dwarf conifers, heathers and alpines.

The old walled vegetable garden on the west side of the house was once home to the children's ponies. Recently it has become Mr Ward-Thomas's domain and he is turning it into an arboretum. There are maples (*Acer hersii* with marbled bark, *A. griseum*, the paperbark maple, and *A. platanoides* 'Drummondii'– a Norway maple cultivar with white margined leaves); crab apples (*Malus* 'John Downie' and 'Golden Hornet' and *M. tschonoskii* – a strong growing tree with splendid autumn colouring of orange, purple and scarlet), a poplar with variegated leaves, *Populus candicans* 'Aurora' and a willow, *Salix alba argentea*, remarkable for its striking silver leaves. Among the trees there are groups of shrubs including potentillas, philadelphuses, cotoneasters, viburnums, berberis and the rose 'Frühlingsgold'.

Gardening is complete relaxation for Mrs Ward-Thomas when she is writing a book and is the perfect antidote to hours spent over the typewriter. She tries to write every day, escaping into the garden when she has finished. There are projects they would still like to tackle – a hidden red border and a Tudor knot garden – but their principle is to make the garden easier to manage. One day they hope to hand over Horham to their children. Mrs Ward-Thomas is anxious that they should receive it in an impeccable condition requiring the minimum of upkeep. Fortunately there are signs that the next generation may be as keen gardeners as their parents. One daughter has begun asking her mother's advice about her own newly acquired garden. The days of 'growing mud' are long gone.

# Sir Nigel Broackes in Oxfordshire

*A*S ONE MIGHT EXPECT of a man whose success in business has made him the Managing Director of a multi-national company employing 50,000 people, Sir Nigel Broackes has exacting standards in his garden. As the garden in question has 15 acres under intensive cultivation and a further 25 acres of woodland, it is fortunate that Sir Nigel and Lady Broackes have an instinctive love of gardening on a grand scale.

When they bought the house at Checkendon in 1980, the first priority was to retrieve the woodland from its jungle of nettles and undergrowth. Sir Nigel says that he is deeply affected by his surroundings; beautiful houses and gardens being an absolute necessity for his contentment. His love of architecture and fine gardens began when he was at school at Stowe. Latterly he has been lucky enough to be able to indulge this passion by living in three country houses, each with a notable garden. The first was Wargrave Manor, which belonged to Gertrude Jekyll's parents for several years. The second was the Deanery at Sonning – a Lutyens house with a Jekyll garden whose influence is obvious in the third, their present house at Checkendon. The site of a dwelling since 1030, the house dates from 1620 with several additions, most recently in 1982. Its grounds are divided into six main parts: the drive, the pond and Elizabethan bowling green, the lawn and shrubberies, the herbaceous walk, the woodland and the kitchen garden. It is immaculately kept by four gardeners but Sir Nigel and Lady Broackes take all the 'executive' decisions. It is a garden of varying elements, formal and wild, but with a strong sense of order throughout. Lady Broackes says, with a smile, that this is due to her husband's influence as he is meticulous in everything he does.

The entrance drive to the north-east of the house is flanked by an avenue of clipped Irish yews; a dramatic approach to the garden which hints at its more formal elements. In contrast, a small pond to one side of the drive is almost surrounded by a coppice. Recently, a rustic bridge was built to give access to the island in the middle of the pond. It has been planted with weeping cherries and hollies. Wisterias, placed at either end of the bridge, are being trained to thread through the rails. The rest of the woodland Sir Nigel now describes as 'tamed' after all the effort put into its clearing and replanting. The old rhododendrons had to be untangled as they were 'choking each other to death' and new azaleas were added to provide colour at the entrance to the wood beyond the herbaceous borders. Today the massive beech trees are largely free of nettles and the glades are carpeted with bracken, foxgloves and feathery grasses.

Beyond the pond, a vast flat lawn, believed to be an Elizabethan bowling

Wild and formal elements mix
with great harmony at
Checkendon Court.

Facing page

Top: Clipped Irish yews along the drive give a foretaste of the formal structure elsewhere in the garden.

Left: Sir Nigel and Lady Broackes at the entrance to the sunken garden.

Right: A wrought-iron gate leads into the woods where the rhododendrons used to 'choke each other to death'.

green, is separated from the drive by yew hedges and half way down its length there is a clipped box avenue which encircles a statue of a woodman and his dog. On the far side of the bowling green a long beech hedge runs from east to west forming the northern boundary of the garden. A holly hedge runs parallel to it and the resulting passage between the two hedges is thought to have been an Elizabethan archery alley.

To the east of the house lies a formal courtyard garden, hidden from the drive by ornate brick and flint walls. The basic form of this garden existed when the Broackeses arrived, but they have put in the low walls, steps and paths which give it definition and style. Sir Nigel is particularly pleased with the new pergola which runs the length of the terrace opposite the drawing room windows. Its design is copied from an Elizabethan painting in the Victoria & Albert Museum called 'The Melancholy Man' which he greatly admires. The pergola is made of African Iroko wood – 'The poor man's mahogany', Sir Nigel calls it – and its elegant balustraded arches are draped with *Clematis montana grandiflora*, the vine *Vitis coignetiae* and the rose 'Albertine'. Two large bushes of the fragrant rugosa rose 'Roseraie de l'Hay' stand on either side of the central arch. Below the pergola the ingeniously designed series of paths, steps and walls surround a sunken garden at whose centre is a rectangular pool. Water falls into this pool from a second pool above it and stone water nymphs, urns and box trees clipped into drum shapes complete a very effective formal arrangement. The beds within the sunken garden and at the base of the courtyard walls are filled with bedding plants twice a year, in spring and summer. 12,000 annuals are used in these schemes and elsewhere in the garden. Some are bought in but most, including pansies, wall-flowers and forget-me-nots, are raised from seed in the greenhouses. The theme changes from year to year. In the spring, for example, there may be tulips and forget-me-nots mixed with perennials like hellebores and Solomon's seal. In summer, standard fuchsias, gloxinias and petunias may be added to the roses and lilies (*L. regale* and *L. candidum*) and evergreen shrubs such as mahonias and cotoneasters which form the permanent structure of the perimeter beds. On the north wall of the courtyard a wisteria frames a garden door and honeysuckles, smoke bushes (*Cotinus coggygria*), viburnums and a

Mixed shrub borders along the croquet lawn.

beauty bush (*Kolkwitzia amabilis*) look well against the brickwork.

A door in the south wall leads to the croquet lawn garden. On the eastern side of this door there is an island shrub bed and a mixed border running along the wall. The shrubbery has two of the best rugosa roses, the white semi-double 'Blanc Double de Coubert' and 'Frau Dagmar Hastrup' with flesh-pink flowers and cream-coloured stamens. The pink and white theme is continued with several viburnums including *V.* x *burkwoodii* and *V. plicatum* 'Mariesii'. There is also *Spiraea thunbergii* – the earliest spiraea to flower – and the variegated dogwood *Cornus alba* 'Elegantissima'. Honeysuckles and clematises grow on the opposite wall and in the border, poppies, lady's mantle, lilies, lupins and foxgloves mingle informally. An unusual shrub in this border is the lime-hating *Leucothoë fontanesiana* with its white flowers hung on arching branches.

Beyond these borders, a small circular rose bed is planted with bushes of the recently introduced HT, 'Silver Jubilee'. A small pavilion covered in climbing roses and a semi-circular hedge of clipped yew screen the swimming pool. The yew makes an attractive backdrop for four classical figures round the pool. On a small lawn near the pavilion there is an effectively placed weeping beech (*Fagus sylvatica* 'Pendula'). At the far end of the croquet lawn a large bush of the rose 'Nevada' is seen in a group of Japanese maples including the striking golden-leaved *Acer palmatum* 'Aureum'. Across the lawn, towards the kitchen garden, a huge beech partly shades a small orchard where cherries and apples grow in long grass. The walls of the house on this side are covered with white and yellow climbing roses and ceanothuses and figs grow in the shelter of an adjoining out-building.

Tall double yew hedges with topiary ornaments form the boundary to the south side of the croquet lawn. Within their shelter two long newly planted

The statue at the centre of the Elizabethan bowling green is surrounded by hedges of clipped yew and box.

Left: The sunken garden seen from the house.

Right: The iroko-wood pergola is draped with *Clematis montana* 'Grandiflora'. The rugosa rose 'Roseraie de l'Hay' peeps through the arches.

herbaceous borders contain a wide range of perennials – phloxes, columbines, dicentras, delphiniums, senecios, paeonies, campanulas, mallows, lilies, hostas, Solomon's seal, Japanese anemones and young buddleias and philadelphuses. The Broackeses' aim is to have flowers throughout the year for arrangements in their houses both in the country and in London. The borders have as wide a variety of plants as possible to extend the flowering season and the greenhouses are well stocked with tender plants and orchids. At one end of the herbaceous borders there is a seat from which to admire them, and at the other there is a small spring garden with statues and naturalised daffodils and bluebells.

On the far side of the hedges, a grass 'pavement' edges the ha-ha which divides the garden from the parkland beyond. From the spring garden at one end of the herbaceous borders, a gate leads into the woods and a woodland path leads back into the kitchen garden west of the croquet lawn. The large quartered beds of the vegetable garden are edged with rustic fences and a central grass path is flanked by borders of mixed perennials and flowers for cutting. This layout, and the surrounding hedges, were probably made in the 1920s when the house was extended and the cottages were built in the yard beyond. A small studio, perfectly in keeping with the other buildings, has been built recently and here Sir Nigel pursues his hobby of gold- and silver-smithing.

Away from the demands of his business life, Sir Nigel says that he enjoys 'being a recluse at home'. Both in the country and in London, even on the coldest of days, he always walks in the garden after work. 'It's not so much that it relieves the stress,' he says, 'rather it helps to sort out the priorities.' The garden at Checkendon is perfection for him. He finds classical 18th-century landscape boring, without enough variety for his taste. His own beautifully tended garden provides an environment that is both stimulating and peaceful.

# Robin Hanbury-Tenison in Cornwall

*A*N EXPLORER SUCH AS Robin Hanbury-Tenison has to be doggedly persistent, endlessly patient and frequently inventive if he is to survive the challenge of his journeys. There can be little doubt that Mr Hanbury-Tenison possesses these qualities. What is surprising is that they are the ones which have also led him to create his extremely original garden in Cornwall.

He came to Cornwall in 1960 when he bought a hill-farm at Maidenwell on Bodmin Moor. It was love at first sight; not only for the wild landscape but also for its curious Spanish-style house – a glorious folly of a hacienda built around an old farmhouse by the previous owner. Mr Hanbury-Tenison was quite undaunted by the prospect of living at 800ft with nothing between him and 'the 17th floor of the Empire State building'. He says that he has never 'sheltered behind the safe walls of convention' and so the idea of living and farming in this rather inhospitable place appealed to him. His wife, Louella, shares his passion for Maidenwell and works with him on the farm and in the garden. Mrs Hanbury-Tenison comes from a family of Cornish gardeners, the famous Williamses of Caerhays and Wherrington.

There was no garden at Maidenwell when Mr Hanbury-Tenison came – 'just a mass of Nissen huts'. He realised that if there was ever to be one he would have to provide shelter and create a more congenial environment. He therefore planted 20 acres of trees, mostly conifers, to the south and west of the house and, as he puts it, waited. The moor has its own fickle climate with a persistent wind, sudden blanketing fogs and rapidly fluctuating temperatures, and even with the shelter of trees, developing the garden has been a difficult task. Mr Hanbury-Tenison has always believed that it is better 'to tame nature rather than to fight against it' and so the garden was planned to fit in with the surrounding landscape, and plants chosen that would tolerate the acid soil. Lying on a south-facing slope below the house, the garden takes its shape from the natural contours and uses to best advantage the springs that rise here.

A walled enclosure adjoining the house provides shelter for soft fruit and vegetables and this is where the head-gardener, Peter, has his greenhouses. But the principal part of the garden lies open to the moor and its most striking feature is the water garden created about 20 years ago. Like a sinuous backbone to the garden, it was made in a rocky gully where 3,000-year-old springs were channelled to cascade over rocks and through a series of dams and pools down into the valley below the garden.

A large area of lawn in front of the house slopes gently down towards the

Mr and Mrs Hanbury-Tenison
in the greenhouses at
Maidenwell.

water garden and at its centre there is a circular pool with a fountain. Below this the lawn drops away sharply to the top of the water garden where the spring starts its descent. At present, existing plants bordering the cascade are being lifted, the soil treated and fed, and the plants replaced. The benefit is evident in their vigorous growth and it allows a broader range of plants to be added as the soil becomes more neutral. The first 'drop' has been planted with a striking mixture of foliage plants and moisture-loving flowering plants. Rodgersias mingle with *Primula florindae* which has self-sown all the way down the cascade. Day lilies, ligularias and astilbes of various kinds make a fine foreground to bamboos. Trees are very important to Mr Hanbury-Tenison and he has done a tremendous amount of planting at Maidenwell. Climbers, especially clematises, grow up any suitable wall or tree; the mature oaks in the area of the water garden are hung with *Clematis montana*. A graceful weeping Japanese larch (*Larix kaempferi* 'Pendula') casts its feathery shadows over a fine stone greyhound which sits at the base of the first cascade, and beside it a *Eucryphia* x *nymansensis* has survived several bad winters. Both sides of the slopes of the water garden have been planted with specimen trees and shrubs. There is a brilliant pairing of a weeping pear (*Pyrus salicifolia* 'Pendula') with a deep-purple berberis (*B. thunbergii atropurpurea*), and there are maples, birches, viburnums and mahonias. A natural stony outcrop reveals the face of Ruth carved from a stone, beneath a hawthorn. The cascade tumbles into a shallow pool beside which there is a pergola. This pool is edged with ferns, rodgersias and arum lilies, with willows, oaks and a *Viburnum plicatum tomentosum* behind. Throughout the garden, the water produces a play of light and shadow and reflects the lushness

Himalayan balsam (*Impatiens glandulifera*) and water irises (*I. pseudacorus*) thrive in the water garden.

Left: A stone greyhound sits proudly at the base of the first 'drop' in the water garden.

Right: The water garden is like 'a sinuous backbone'. At its top, spring water gushes from a lead fish's mouth.

of the surrounding plants, giving it a jungle-like quality.

The water then flows under a narrow causeway and drops into the pond below, which is filled with water irises (*I. pseudacorus*) and Himalayan balsam (*Impatiens glandulifera*). On one side a rustic pergola is covered with the honeysuckle *Lonicera japonica* 'Halliana'. Recently, the lowest pool has been reclaimed from the undergrowth to reveal the gunneras, rodgersias and rheums which flank it and the stream which trickles on into the valley. This final pool has a charming statue of a boy holding a dolphin and a clump of an unidentified rare white iris given to the Hanbury-Tenisons by Beth Chatto.

Beyond the water garden, a path follows the course of the stream, passing into the shade of the larch and Norway spruce that screen this area. There are plans to make a water-meadow garden in the marshy valley below and to excavate further along the valley to form a lake with an island. Mr Hanbury-Tenison wants to create a balanced landscape which both man and wildlife can enjoy. With these expansions, the garden will eventually cover 25 acres.

On a slope just west of the water garden is a group of 'weeping' trees – a rowan (*Sorbus aucuparia* 'Pendula'), the willow *Salix caprea* 'Kilmarnock' and a winter-flowering cherry (*Prunus subhirtella pendula*). Two quinces 'weep' over a seat which overlooks the lower part of the water garden. To the east, a new plantation of trees and shrubs is taking shape. Here, there is an emphasis on elegance of outline and rich autumn colour. The trees include the white-barked birch (*Betula jacquemontii*), the willow *Salix matsudana* 'Tortuosa', the aspen (*Populus tremula*), rowans for their autumn colour (*Sorbus aucuparia* and *S. vilmoriniana*), cypress-oak (*Quercus robur fastigiata*), the katsura tree (*Cercidiphyl-*

*lum japonicum*) which has outstanding autumn colour and a snowdrop tree (*Halesia diptera*). These are underplanted with many kinds of shrubs – spiraeas, cistuses, potentillas, enkianthus and the beauty-berry (*Callicarpa bodinieri* 'Profusion'). Mr Hanbury-Tenison is a firm believer in 'controlled gardening' and this new area will eventually become one with the countryside beyond, with no visible boundary. The Hanbury-Tenisons started with no preconceptions about their garden and have learnt as they went along, with the excellent advice of Peter and of the under-gardener, David. They love the unglamorous side of gardening and spend hours clearing for new planting.

A new heather and conifer bed has been made near the plantation and Peter has taken hundreds of cuttings to increase stock. In the walled garden he has built a series of interconnecting greenhouses where he grows a wide range of flowers – including orchids – for the house. Cuttings are nurtured in large cold-frames and a compact vegetable garden supplies seakale, mangetouts, artichokes and other unusual things. 'We don't grow Brussels sprouts as they cost out at about £1 each!' says Mr Hanbury-Tenison.

On the eastern side of the house, facing the lawn, an attempt has been made to plant a traditional mixed border of oriental poppies, rugosa roses, sedums, pinks, lupins and lavender. But the soil and weather do not really suit them. On the western side of the lawn, above the water garden, a broad shrubbery is planted with the plants that do so well here – mainly rhododendrons and azaleas. This border is continually being improved and 100 new rhododendron hybrids are waiting to be planted.

The Hanbury-Tenisons respect and understand the wildlife around them and are determined to get the balance right between man and nature both on the farm and in their garden. They involve themselves in a practical way in nature conservation and Mr Hanbury-Tenison has tried very hard to stop badger-gassing locally. On their 1000-acre farm they raise sheep, cattle, angora goats and deer. To round up their livestock they use the Camargue ponies that they rode back from France specifically for that purpose.

Robin Hanbury-Tenison has not yet instigated a botanical expedition. He immensely enjoyed one particular journey through South America with 180 researchers when 150 new species of plants and animals were discovered. He says that expeditions are usually 5% pleasure, 90% tedium and 5% hell. He adds that the greatest appeal of going away is the prospect of coming home and he looks forward to being able to spend most of the year at Maidenwell.

Gunneras, rodgersias and rheums were revealed when the lowest pool was cleared. Beth Chatto's large white iris is on the right.

Top: Throughout the garden the Hanbury-Tenisons have encouraged a balance between the wild and the cultivated species. As here in and around the pool on the lawn above the water garden.

Bottom: The sweeping lawn with water garden below and sheltering trees beyond. The garden is open to the moor which can be seen in the distance.

101

# Barbara Cartland in Hertfordshire

*B*ARBARA CARTLAND'S ESTATE, covering 400 acres of rural Hertford-shire, would make a perfect setting for one of her romantic novels. The scale of the landscape with its ancient meadows, trees, lakes and woodland walks inspires thoughts of a vanished age. A house was first built on the site in 1275 by a knight reputed to have been called Camfield or Camfeld. During Elizabeth I's reign, a fine manor house with formal gardens was built and this remained intact until 1867, when Beatrix Potter's grandfather bought the estate. He pulled down the Elizabethan house and replaced it with the spacious Victorian house that has been Miss Cartland's home since 1950.

The house stands on a hill overlooking a wooded valley at the bottom of which are two small lakes. The view is breathtaking and much loved by Miss Cartland. A Roman road runs through the estate and the small bridge which spans the lakes' connecting stream is supposed to be part of it. Large lawns surround the house and fall away in front of the terrace to the meadows beyond. A previous owner, Lord Queensborough, was a keen plantsman and to the north and west of the house masses of rhododendrons, azaleas, yews, philadelphuses, lilacs and other shrubs attest to his interest. A large walled vegetable garden lies to the east of the house and its walls are all that remain of the formal Elizabethan garden. This was the setting for Beatrix Potter's story of Peter Rabbit – Mr MacGregor's garden. As a child Beatrix Potter lived in South Kensington with her parents, and it must have been a delight for her to escape to the Hertfordshire countryside to visit her grandparents. She spent hours walking and playing in the garden, a rather lonely little girl, taking in everything around her. When, as a young woman, she wrote to the sick child of Frederick Warne, her friend and later her publisher, she included sketches and the story of Peter Rabbit. Warne was so impressed that he persuaded her to make the story into a book. Naturally, she chose to set it in the garden she knew and loved best – that of her grandparents. Miss Cartland has tried to preserve the vegetable garden as much as possible. The door in the wall that the little rabbit was too fat to squeeze underneath is still there. So is the pond where the white cat sat and watched the goldfish. The rabbits are still there too and Miss Cartland's gardeners have a constant struggle to stop them eating young trees and shrubs.

Miss Cartland was born in Worcestershire and her earliest memories are of Pershore plum orchards. She remembers well the first time that the outside world impressed itself upon her. Out for a walk with her nanny, she 'suddenly became aware of flowers all around her in the meadow – daisies, buttercups and wild orchids'. It was the beginning of her lasting love of flowers. Now she says

The pool on the far side of the wood never fails to inspire Barbara Cartland.

103

she 'cannot live without being surrounded by them' in her house. Madonna lilies (*Lilium candidum*) are her favourites and her son Ian grows them specially for her in his own garden. Every week fresh flowers are arranged for the house and Miss Cartland loves 'large, informal country-house arrangements'.

Working as hard as she does at her writing every day, Miss Cartland finds her garden an essential part of her life. Nowhere else can she derive the same inspiration and collect her thoughts together for her writing. Miss Cartland has travelled extensively throughout her life but does not like to be away from Camfield for too long and on her return the first thing she does is to take a walk around her garden. At the far side of the wood to the west of the house a circular pool is surrounded by sheltering trees. Her son Glen has planted a collection of foliage plants within a natural arrangement of moss-covered rocks. Plants which now thrive in the moist soil of the pond's bank are the hostas *H. crispula* and *H. fortunei* 'Aureomarginata', a variety of ferns including the fine shuttlecock form *Matteucia struthiopteris*, the yellow iris (*I. pseudacorus*) and an ornamental rhubarb *Rheum alexandrae*. This border was much admired by Beverley Nichols when he visited Camfield shortly before he died. It gives immense pleasure to Miss Cartland. Twice a day she walks her dogs through the wood to the pool and sits on a seat at its edge; in the morning before she starts writing and again in the afternoon when she has finished. It is in this special and beautiful place that many of the ideas for her writing come to her.

In the wood near the pond is an enormous oak. During the reign of Mary I, her younger half-sister Elizabeth was imprisoned at Hatfield House which is the neighbouring estate to Camfield. It is said that one day while out hunting, Elizabeth killed her first stag with a cross-bow. To commemorate the event, she planted an oak where it fell. The oak in Miss Cartland's wood is that tree. She

Left: The door in the wall of the kitchen garden under which Peter Rabbit was 'too fat to squeeze'.

Right: Miss Cartland's 'magic tree'; an oak reputed to have been planted by Elizabeth I.

Miss Cartland's parasol glimpsed over the irises that fringe her favourite pool.

calls it her 'Magic Tree' and every year acorns and leaves are collected from it and dipped in gold. Miss Cartland gives them to her friends and they are reputed to bring the recipients good luck. In early summer the heady fragrance of the many philadelphuses planted in this part of the wood adds to the magic.

A favourite tree of Miss Cartland's is the enormous cedar (*Cedrus libani*) on the edge of the drive, which is the first feature of the garden to catch the visitor's eye. It is over 200 years old and in fine condition. A mature tulip tree (*Liriodendron tulipifera*) and a blue cedar (*Cedrus atlantica glauca*) are worthy companions to it on either side of the drive. Throughout the 35 years that Miss Cartland and her family have lived at Camfield they have sought to make the garden easier to manage. Miss Cartland has been instrumental in introducing low-maintenance shrub and tree borders. In the past, twelve full-time gardeners were employed but now there are only three and sometimes one or two of these are whisked away to help with other jobs on the estate.

Across the lawn behind the house a small Gothic folly built in 1750 has always been a popular spot for children to play. From here the north side of the house can be appreciated, with an enormous Virginia creeper and *Magnolia grandiflora* clothing the stonework. A yew tree covered in honeysuckle is the focal point of the lawn in the summer, its colour complementing the pelargoniums in the formal beds by the house. A pets' graveyard is situated near the folly. Miss Cartland's animals are another essential part of her life and even when they die 'I like to know that they are near me,' she says.

Miss Cartland does not have much time in her busy life to visit other gardens. She is really only truly happy in her own, and her late husband Hugh loved it above all other places. It is not only a source of inspiration and solace to her but it is also full of memories.

# Simon Hornby
# in Oxfordshire

IT IS A WIDELY HELD BELIEF that no one begins to garden until they are well into middle age. Simon Hornby, the Chairman of W.H.Smith & Son, is the exception that proves the rule. Gardening has always been part of his life. His parents bought Pusey House in 1936 and, after the Second World War, began creating their famous garden – undoubtedly one of the finest gardens made in England since the War. Mr Hornby started gardening when he was a boy, to help his parents, although he says that he was never put under any pressure to do so; he just found that he enjoyed it. His interest in plants must have started early because he remembers 'nipping over the wall' into the Savill Garden while he was a schoolboy at Eton and being transfixed by its beauty, particularly by the Himalayan poppies of the sharpest blue and primulas which seemed bigger and more exotic than any that he had seen before or since. He was so entranced by the polyanthuses he saw there that he used to 'steal' the seeds to take home to his parents. It was the beginning of an interest that has endured; collecting seed and throwing it about the garden is still a favourite pastime.

He describes his garden as a cottage garden and himself as a Jekyll-style gardener and professes not to be a plantsman. His garden covers about one acre and is totally his own creation. With parents who are such skilled gardeners, it would have been easy just to ask their advice and to use their garden as the source of all the plants for his own, especially as they live next door, but Mr Hornby was determined not to do that. He wanted his garden to reflect his own ideas and to be filled with his own choice of plants. He started work on it in 1970, having decided to concentrate on the small front garden and the walled rectangular plot directly behind the house. It was several years before he found the time to make the water garden at the far end of the main garden. In 1980 he began to cultivate the second rear garden which lies parallel to the first, separated from it by a stone wall. Today the whole of his garden is a remarkable example of what can be achieved in a fairly limited space with excellent planning, a strong aesthetic sense and a profound love and knowledge of plants.

When Mr and Mrs Hornby bought their Georgian farmhouse not only did it need a great deal of repair but the garden was a wilderness. This pleased them for it meant that they could remodel the farmhouse to their own requirements and, above all, Mr Hornby could plan the garden without the constraints of any previous owner's planting. The only trees were some elderly apples which he decided to keep. It did not take him long to discover that the garden had poor soil and that it would take some time before it was rid of weeds. Even after sixteen years, the soil is still a problem and, despite lavish feeding every year, certain

Simon Hornby surrounded by plants on the terrace of his house.

plants just will not thrive in it. Lilies never do well and, much to Mr Hornby's regret, many plants which he would like to seed about the garden simply refuse to perform. He hand-weeded all the beds for two years before he planted anything, a practice he thoroughly recommends for, since then, perennial weeds have never been much of a problem.

In planning the small entrance garden Mr Hornby decided to keep to a simple idea and to make only one large bed opposite the house near the boundary hedge. He planted it to provide berries and hips. In it are some of his favourite roses like the rugosa 'Belle Poitevine', which he grows from cuttings, and the species *R. sweginzowii*, *R. glauca* (formerly known as *R. rubrifolia*) and *R. moyesii* 'Geranium', all of which have striking hips: Here, also, he put two of what he thinks of as the best viburnums – *V. x hillieri*, a semi-evergreen with bronze-tinged leaves in winter, and *V. betulifolium* with its red-currant like berries. There is also the cotoneaster, *C.* 'Exburiensis Rothschildianus' – a large shrub with creamy-yellow berries, and the crab apple 'Professor Sprenger' which has amber-coloured fruit.

On either side of the steps leading to the front door, there are rectangular raised beds where he has trained bushes of the exquisite rose 'Louise Odier' to cascade over the retaining walls. It has cupped flowers, warm pink with a touch of lilac, and a delicious scent. Among the rose bushes are soft lilac violas, the grey-leaved *Anaphalis triplinervis* and the charming blue bindweed *Convolvulus sabatius* (syn. *C. mauritanicus*). On this wall of the house are several climbing roses – flourishing despite being on a north wall; they include 'Gloire de Dijon', 'Madame Caroline Testout' and 'Paul's Lemon Pillar'.

At the back of the house there are more climbing roses – 'Lady Waterlow' and 'Mermaid'. Here a raised terrace separates the garden from the house. On this terrace, lead troughs are filled with marguerites in summer, and large tubs with agapanthus which thrive in this hot spot. From the middle of the terrace steps lead down to the lawn at the heart of the garden. On the lawn, two rows of standard 'Iceberg' roses lead the eye to the far end of the garden and the farmland beyond. Below the terrace a pair of matching borders, of shrubs and perennials, have a major theme of white. Here is the dwarf shrub x *Halimiocistus*

Left: Climbing roses surround the front door and raised beds are planted with silver-leaved plants and the rose 'Louise Odier'.

Right: The back of the house and the lawn with its standard 'Iceberg' roses seen from the far end of the shady western border.

Top: Soft colours emphasise the tranquillity of the water garden.

Bottom: The herbaceous border which was the first bed to be planted by Mr Hornby.

'Ingwersenii', a natural hybrid discovered in Portugal by Ingwersen in 1929. It resembles a cistus and bears its pure white flowers over a very long season. Nearby, an old apple tree provides support for the climbing rose 'Blairi No 2'. This lovely rose, introduced in 1845, has true old rose flowers, deep pink at the centre becoming paler towards the edge.

A gravel path runs along the east side of the lawn and divides it from a wide herbaceous border. This was the first bed to be planted by Mr Hornby and it still contains many of its original treasures. It is backed by an old stone wall which provides the home for some much loved roses and clematises. The uncommon white-flowered rose 'Mrs Herbert Stevens' associates happily with a favourite clematis, the lavender-blue flowered 'Mrs Cholmondeley'. Although this border contains every colour of the spectrum, the plants have been so skilfully chosen and placed that the effect is charmingly pretty. There are many of the traditional herbaceous border plants – hollyhocks, monkshoods, irises, campanulas, cranesbills – but in each case Mr Hornby has chosen what he believes to be the best variety. He grows the Chinese monkshood *Aconitum carmichaelii* with pale, Wedgwood blue flowers and glossy foliage; the oriental poppy *Papaver orientale* 'Ladybird', with its rich vermilion flowers blotched with black; his favourite bearded iris, 'Jane Phillips', with large pale-blue flowers. At the far end of the border there is the very effective association of the white flowered form of abutilon (*A. vitifolium alba*), with the uncommon pale yellow foxglove (*Digitalis lutea*). Standing out among the cranesbills is the tall, magenta flowered *Geranium psilostemon*. At the end of the border nearest the house is a large Jerusalem sage (*Phlomis fruticosa*), the annual red orach (*Atriplex hortensis* – a prolific seeder which is found throughout the border) and the Russian sage (*Perovskia atriplicifolia* 'Blue Spire'). As well as the wide colour range in this border there is

Left: A corner of the new garden planted since 1980. *Vitis coignetiae* and climbing roses smother one wall.

Right: In the western border of the rear garden yellow, white and silver plants are used to great effect. Welsh poppies (*Papaver cambrica*) are mixed with *Dorycnium hirsutum* and a white *Dicentra formosa*. In the foreground are the grey feathery leaves of *Tanacetum haradjanii*.

110

The lovely paeony 'Duchesse de Nemours' and pink lavender at the entrance to the water garden.

also great diversity of leaf form and texture. At the back, giant mulleins with 10ft high spikes of yellow flowers intermingle with the huge white clouds of *Crambe cordifolia*. At the front of the border an onion with flower heads like 'pink tennis balls' (*Allium albopilosum*), grows to great effect among columbines, aquilegias, tradescantias and cranesbills.

On the western side of the terrace, at lawn level, there is a paved area for sitting. Walled on three sides and open to the south, this provides an ideally protected site for the magnificent shrub *Carpenteria californica*. With its glossy foliage and large single white flowers it is, when in flower, probably Mr Hornby's favourite plant. Here too is the striking climber *Actinidia kolomikta*, with large pink-edged leaves. In the paving, gaps have been left to accommodate rock roses, lady's mantle, aubretias, self-sown spurges, Welsh poppies and red valerian. From this sitting area an irregularly shaped border leads to an old stone outbuilding half way down the west side. This border, backed by a stone wall has at its house end an old well-head surrounded by honeysuckle, with bushes of the rose 'Gruss an Aachen' growing nearby. Near the outbuilding one of the original cherry trees provides summer shade. Here are tree paeonies, evergreen viburnums, the hydrangea *H. sargentiana*, hellebores, hostas ('Honeybells' is his favourite), spurges, pink cow-parsley and *Actaea rubra*, a perennial with attractive leaves and red berries in late summer.

Mr Hornby is a great admirer of Margery Fish's writing and, like her, he loves to see all his borders enormously full. He firmly believes in nature being given a fairly free rein and so loves to find plants that have sown themselves. Despite his long experience of gardening, and the fact that he writes a regular gardening column for *The Tatler*, Mr Hornby claims that he has no 'scholarly knowledge'. He thinks his only skills as a gardener lie in his ability to plan, to arrange

111

interesting plant associations and 'to make things grow'. The water garden, at the far end of the main garden, demonstrates all these skills beautifully. It is a small paved rectangle with a central circular pool and a fountain and entirely surrounded with a hedge of *Cotoneaster lacteus*. The colour range has been restricted to white, pink and blue with a hint of yellow in the lady's mantle around the fountain. Water lilies cover the pool and the beds show a profusion of roses, honeysuckles, paeonies, weigelas and philadelphuses. At the height of the season it is extremely effective – a generous exuberance of carefully chosen colour with delicious scent. Among the roses there is the uncommon hybrid musk 'Lavender Lassie' which has double rosette flowers – pink shading to lavender – and a marvellous scent. Here too is the dwarf philadelphus with double flowers, 'Manteau d'Hermine', and the delectable white paeony 'Duchesse de Nemours'. The paths are fringed with bushes of pink lavender underplanted with irises of the softest blue and the white *Viola cornuta* 'Alba'. False indigo *(Baptisia australis)* grows well here too, with its dark-blue flowers resembling sweet-peas, together with another of Mr Hornby's favourite cranesbills *Geranium pratense* 'Mrs Kendall Clark', with pale silvery blue flowers.

Between the water garden and the shady border a narrow path leads through to the new garden, completely planted since 1980. Against the far side of the wall, just inside the gate, there is an iris bed with many plants trained against the wall. Among these are the silver-leaved *Buddleia fallowiana* 'Alba', a purple flowered berry, *Rubus odoratus*, and the clematis *C. alpina* 'Frances Rivis'. An Indian bean tree *(Catalpa bignonioides)* is planted in the gravel by the gate, surrounded with the geranium *G. wlassovianum* A small lawn nearby is edged

Facing page: Dazzling colour in the new garden with *Papaver orientale* 'Ladybird' in the foreground.

Outside the water garden a paeony hedge borders one side of the old orchard.

with wild strawberries, a white campanula ( *C. posharskyana* 'E.H.Frost') and the cranesbill *Geranium clarkei* 'Kashmir White'. At one side of the lawn a stone seat is flanked by what Mr Hornby calls 'the best bergenia', *B. crassifolia*, and behind there is a group of mahonias and the vigorous variegated Himalayan comfrey (*Symphytum uplandicum* 'Variegatum'). From the seat a narrow path leads between double mixed borders to the top of the garden where there is another sitting area. In these borders the emphasis is on shrubs. Near the stone seat yellows predominate, blending well with the whites about the the lawn. Gradually the colours change to pinks, purples and reds. In the yellow section, plume poppies (*Macleaya cordata*) intermingle with golden elder (*Sambucus racemosa* 'Plumosa Aurea'), a golden ribes and a golden rubus. Further along, roses are mixed with buddleias, deutzias, mahonias and osmanthuses and a few favourite herbaceous plants. The effect is luxuriant and informal.

Over the sixteen years that Mr Hornby has spent making his garden he has done much of the work himself. He says that he enjoys all the jobs and would not be happy leaving it to someone else. Despite all this effort, he is not sentimental about it and would be perfectly happy to start all over again – 'to get away from what everyone grows'. He feels that, generally, gardeners are not sufficiently courageous or experimental; they tend to play safe and stick with plants that they know. As a result their gardens lack originality and style. Hr Hornby's own appetite for gardening is as sharp as ever, his palate unjaded, and he says that he cannot wait for the day he retires; when he will be able to do nothing but 'garden and listen to Mozart'.

# John Makepeace
# in Dorset

A S ENGLAND'S LEADING FURNITURE MAKER John Makepeace believes in fostering excellence. It is the philosophy behind the Parnham
Trust and the School for Craftsmen in Wood which he founded at
Parnham House in Dorset in 1977. Standards of excellence are integral to the
restoration of the garden at Parnham. Mrs Makepeace is, according to her
husband, the gardener. Her contribution to the garden has been enormous but
she feels that without her husband's help and advice she would have been lost.
He is the one with bold architectural ideas, she the plantswoman. Together they
have done much to restore the garden to the days of its Edwardian splendour
when 18 gardeners looked after it.

Before coming to Parnham Mr Makepeace had a workshop in Oxfordshire
where, with a growing reputation, he found himself under pressure to take on
students. He saw Parnham and knew it would be the perfect place to start a
school. The site of a dwelling since 1400, the house has undergone all sorts of
alterations. Earlier this century its Elizabethan interiors were restored and the
gardens remodelled, when a courtyard was built on the east side of the house
and a series of terraces on the south. It is set in gentle Dorset countryside and
approached through parkland that was once part of the Parnham estate. At a
bend of the drive near the house, a group of contorted old magnolias are some of
Mr Makepeace's favourite plants on the estate. He believes they are 'Swamp
Bays'(*Magnolia virginiana*). Their sweetly scented blossom appears throughout
the summer.

From the magnolias the drive leads into a courtyard where the beds have been
largely replanted by Mrs Makepeace. Here are many roses which the Makepeaces
love. There are hybrid musks – 'Penelope', 'Felicia' and 'Buff Beauty' – which are
underplanted with the bugle *Ajuga reptans* 'Burgundy Blue', her favourite
herbaceous polygonum *P. affine* 'Donald Lowndes', catmint and chives. The idea
of growing chives among roses came from Gertrude Jekyll; they are decorative
and are supposed to keep greenfly at bay. On the walls behind are several
climbing roses including 'Meg', 'Rosy Mantle', 'Zéphirine Drouhin' and
'Handel'. Two stone pillars near the gates are covered with the rambler
'Albertine' and nearby, 'Constance Spry' is trained on wooden pillars. On the
house wall facing the courtyard there is an enormous *Magnolia* x *soulangiana*,
another of Mr Makepeace's favourite plants. Around Christmas he is to be found
up a ladder pruning it – a job he likes to do himself.

North of the courtyard, in a small walled area by the house, Mrs Makepeace
grows silver and grey plants. She regards it almost as a secret garden. Many of

A statue of Morecambe and
Wise in the woods
at Parnham.

the plants come from the nursery at East Lambrook Manor in Somerset, the home of the late Margery Fish, one of Mrs Makepeace's favourite garden writers. At its heart are a weeping pear (*Pyrus salicifolia* 'Pendula') and bushes of the hortensia hydrangea 'Madame E. Mouillère'. This is a fairly tender variety with white flowers tinged with pink. Among the most attractive of this little garden's many plants are a white dicentra (*D. oregona*) and *Dorycnium hirsutum* with its grey, hairy leaves and pinkish-white flowers.

A gate in the south wall of the courtyard leads to the 'Ladies' Terrace', the first of three terraces which extend along the south and west sides of the house. On this terrace, as with the others, simplicity is the keynote. Wide gravel paths criss-cross lawns whose only ornaments are clipped box and yew trees. At the west end of the 'Ladies' Terrace', Mrs Makepeace has a herb garden where, as an avid collector, she has amassed a wide variety of species, particularly of mints. Here she has also planted the semi-evergreen climber *Akebia quinata* in association with the roses 'Meg' and 'Rosy Mantle' behind a clump of *Iris sibirica*.

On the south side of the house, a wide flight of steps leads from the 'Ladies' Terrace' to the one below. This second terrace is crossed by parallel water channels, fed from a spring, which run down either side of the steps to the third terrace and then disappear underground to flow into the river that marks the boundary on the south and west sides of the garden. Fifty clipped yews are planted in the grass on the second terrace: a simple but bold planting that matches beautifully the grandeur of the house.

Magnificent trees are a feature of Parnham and, as one might expect, are Mr Makepeace's principal interest in the garden. He loves the old Lucombe oaks (*Quercus* x *hispanica* 'Lucombeana') which grow on the western edge of the third terrace near the river. The Makepeaces have planted a line of that most attractive rowan *Sorbus cashmiriana* on the edge of the third terrace. Near the oaks they

Left: Fifty yews arranged symetrically on the second terrace.

Right: Mr and Mrs Makepeace on the steps leading to the second terrace.

Left: One half of the long herbaceous border. The Makepeaces discovered the herringbone brick path under a lawn.

Right: The gateway between the courtyard and Ladies' Terrace.

have put a golden beech (*Fagus sylvatica* 'Zlatia') and a purple beech whose leaves have a pale pink border (*Fagus sylvatica* 'Purpurea Tricolor'). By the river large numbers of red, purple and yellow willows have been added.

Behind the house, a pretty woodland path leads to a shady corner where the Makepeaces are creating a bog garden with moisture-loving plants like ligularias, rodgersias, candelabra primulas and the spectacular *Gunnera manicata*. Deeper into the wood stands an enormous statue of Morecambe and Wise. The Makepeaces enjoy its incongruity in such a setting – and the reactions it produces in their visitors.

In the Italian garden, which lies to the north of the house, the Makepeaces have created a long mixed border. Some of the perennials have been raised from seed and there are treasures passed on by friends. The border is divided into two parts separated by a yew hedge. In one part white, pink, blue and silver plants are mixed and in the other, creams, yellows, oranges and reds. In the paler of the two, a white buddleia (*B. fallowiana alba*) and the glaucous-leaved rose *R. glauca* provide height and background for the hostas, lupins, phloxes, cardoons and other perennials. In the other, there is wintersweet (*Chimonanthus praecox*), the spring flowering doronicums, Oriental poppies, the fine *Alchemilla alpina* and a spectacular spurge, *Euphorbia griffithii* 'Fireglow'. There is contrast provided by the dark-leaved fennel and variegated hawkweed. Copying an idea from Vita Sackville-West, a group of verbascums stands against the yew hedge.

Mr Makepeace says that he is looking forward to the time when he can actually do much more of the labouring in the garden. There are all kinds of projects he wants to tackle himself. At present his work on the Parnham Trust and the School simply do not leave enough time. 'A perfectionist in everything,' says Mrs Makepeace, 'he won't be satisfied until he can put more of his energy into the garden and it achieves the excellence which is the goal in every sphere of his life.'

# Lord Carrington in Buckinghamshire

**D**URING HIS POLITICAL CAREER Lord Carrington held nine posts in government and in opposition before becoming Foreign Secretary in 1979. Following his resignation in 1982 he was made Chairman of GEC and became Secretary General of NATO in 1984. Most people would regard such a life as full of stress; Lord Carrington seems far from weighed down by it and has lost none of his zest for life. At home, the farm and the garden provide him with all the physical activity he needs, and have never failed to provide a refuge from the cares of office. The Carringtons are both avid gardeners and theirs is a gardening partnership of long standing. They have worked together for over 30 years on their garden in Buckinghamshire. Lord Carrington says simply, 'We gradually became obsessed with it'.

When they moved to the house in 1946 they were not gardeners and it was ten years before their interest in the garden began to take hold. Today they are both equally keen though they have different horticultural priorities. Lord Carrington thinks that the lay-out of the garden is all important, whereas his wife is much more interested in individual plants. They both enjoy the physical work that gardening entails and have their favourite jobs. Lord Carrington likes planting and weeding but hates 'the fiddly jobs' such as dead-heading and labelling which he leaves to Lady Carrington. They both choose plants and have firm ideas about how a garden should look. Lord Carrington recalls how, at a stroke, his wife did away with double herbaceous borders and replaced them with one – against his wishes. 'I remain to be convinced that it was a good idea,' he adds with a smile.

Describing the land surrounding their house as flat and uninteresting, they feel that it is especially important to have a beautiful garden. When they began to garden in earnest, they decided to divide the existing rather bland five-acre plot into 'rooms' to produce a series of small intimate gardens, each with its own flavour. They set about planting yew and beech hedges and added to the existing trees. 30 years on, the magnificent hedges and fine specimen trees give the garden a timeless quality that is intensely English.

There are two enclosed gardens on the south side of the house. The larger was made about 20 years ago after fire destroyed an old tithe barn. It was designed by the landscape architect Robert Adam. 'With a name like that, we felt we could not go wrong,' says Lord Carrington. The result is a most satisfying and peaceful little garden on two levels with terraces, pool, lawns and a walk of *Viburnum tomentosum* trained as standards. This is the home of some of the Carringtons' favourite shrub roses which were planted when the garden was made and which, after 20 years are beginning, Lady Carrington feels, to show their age.

The dining-room terrace and
herbaceous borders seen
through a yew archway.

Among them are 'Constance Spry', 'Canary Bird', the Hybrid Musk 'Cornelia', the unusual Gallica 'Hippolyte' with rich purple flowers, and 'Celestial' with semi-double shell-pink flowers and attractive grey foliage. There are also the Sweet Briar 'Lady Penzance' and the Bourbon 'Madame Isaac Péreire'. The modern shrub rose 'Nymphenburg', reputed to have a sweet apple scent, has been placed at one end of the rose border and the roses are underplanted with polyanthuses for spring colour, succeeded by catmint in the summer. Beyond the viburnum walk, a low wall and beech hedge partly screen the pool in the sunken garden. The pool is full of water-lilies and is guarded by two lead herons which peer into the water. In the summer, eight wooden tubs, overflowing with fuchsias, pelargoniums and petunias are placed round the edge. The sloping area beyond the pool is terraced and planted with shrubs. Species roses and ceanothuses tumble over the walls and mix with jasmines and *Cotoneaster horizontalis* planted below. On higher ground to the east of the sunken garden there are two rows of pleached limes and to the west, a summer house designed by Lord Carrington to offset the blankness of the farm-buildings beyond.

Next to this garden, on its east side, there is a tiny paved garden. Here campanulas, pinks (especially the frilly white 'Mrs Sinkins'), gentians and helianthemums flourish in the cracks between the paving stones. A stone urn on a plinth stands at the centre and at each corner are beds with shrubs whose flowers mirror the yellows, blues and whites of the plants in the paving. The Mexican orange (*Choisya ternata*) grows among pale yellow potentillas, *Senecio greyii* and the winter-flowering *Mahonia japonica*. In early summer white paeonies produce delicately scented flowers and the useful ground-covering *Hypericum calycinum* grows under the shrubs. Decorative spurges have been allowed to seed themselves lavishly and, for the summer, white tobacco plants

Lord and Lady Carrington in the sundial garden they created.

are bedded out.

Lord Carrington made the large lawn at the front of the house and planted its specimen trees 35 years ago. Along its north side a long yew hedge runs from the house to the walled kitchen garden near the entrance gate. An opening in the hedge near the house leads into another of the Carringtons' creations – the sundial garden. This is a topiary garden where low box hedges, laid out in a geometric pattern, surround a bronze sundial on a stone pillar. Lord Carrington thinks that this is possibly his favourite bit of the garden but doubts if he would feel the same way about it if he had to clip all the hedges himself!

From here a brick path leads west through another gap in a yew hedge to one of the largest enclosures of the garden. A generous lawn stands at its centre with an old yew tree on the side nearest the sundial garden. Three golden yews, meticulously clipped into ball shapes, provide interest in a dark corner, showing up beautifully against the green yew hedge behind. A narrow border runs along the house on this side, planted with scented shrubs, perennials and dwarf conifers. Philadelphuses (*P. coronarius* 'Aureus', *P.* 'Belle Etoile' and *P.* 'Beauclerk') are trimmed to keep them to a manageable size and prevent them from swamping the roses, daphnes and the winter-flowering *Sarcococca confusa* that are planted among them. A brick path separates this border from wider rectangular ones planted with dwarf shrubs. In front of them a well-established lavender hedge (*Lavandula angustifolia* 'Munstead') fringes the lawn. Beyond the house a wide bed backed by a a wall is planted with flowering shrubs – 15ft philadelphuses, heavy with blossom in their season, tower over escallonias, lilacs, weigelas and *Kolkwitzia amabilis* planted around them. These shrubs are underplanted with hostas, lady's mantle and both blue and white *Campanula persicifolia*.

Clipped balls of golden yew provide dramatic emphasis to a corner of the garden on the north side of the house.

The magnificent paeony and delphinium border in the kitchen garden is one of Lord Carrington's favourite parts of the garden.

The fan garden. Each section, defined in box, is filled with one kind of plant only.

124

Lady Carrington's herbaceous border. She decided that one very wide border would be more effective than two narrower ones.

Lady Carrington's magnificent herbaceous border runs along the side of the lawn opposite the yew tree. Beyond it the farmland can be seen in the distance. To add height at the back of the border there are more philadelphuses, plume poppies (*Macleaya cordata*) and a selection of stunning delphiniums. In accordance with tradition, the plants in the border have been arranged so that colours from the cooler end of the spectrum have been planted at the sides of the border with the most vivid reds and oranges in the centre. At both ends there are ornamental cabbages (*Brassica oleracea capitata*), their whitish leaves flushed with pink. The splendid small white yarrow 'The Pearl' and the white mallow *Malva moschata* 'Alba' grow among them. Yellow yarrows (*Achillea filipendulina* 'Coronation Gold' and 'Gold Plate') mingle with the whites and tickseed planted alongside. The blue-grey *Veronica gentianoides* and the forget-me-not like flowers of *Brunnera macrophylla* go beautifully with the pink paeonies and cranesbills planted towards the middle of the border. In among them are many silver-leaved plants – *Stachys lanata* 'Silver Carpet', artemisias and pinks. In the middle of the border a stone urn overflows with pelargoniums matched in colour by clumps of *Lychnis chalcedonica* and a herbaceous potentilla planted nearby. Bronze-leaved ligularias and *Veratrum nigrum* with its strap-leaves and almost black flower spikes add extra interest of colour and form. Gaps are filled with lady's mantle, lavender, sweet williams and snapdragons. Weaving among them is the valuable

A large enclosed garden where the colour scheme is yellow, white and mauve. Floribunda roses are planted amid masses of lavender.

*Polemonium carneum* which produces its attractive pink flowers from spring to late summer.

Opposite the house on the far side of the lawn a small silver and grey border has been made in the shade of an ash tree. Here white lilacs, the dogwood *Cornus alba* 'Elegantissima', the delicate bridal wreath, *Spiraea* x *arguta* and *Crambe cordifolia* have been mixed with hostas, rue and the woolly-leaved *Ballota pseudodictamnus*. Further along the border there is a lovely mixture of irises and weeping pears (*Pyrus salicifolia* 'Pendula'). The trees help to screen this part of the garden from the road.

A second gap in the hedge behind the clipped golden yews leads into another enclosed garden: a large rectangle where yellow and white roses and lavender have been planted. The roses are floribundas – the white 'Iceberg' and the yellow 'Arthur Bell' and 'Korresia'. Around the edge of this garden are beds of flowering shrubs – viburnums, mahonias and philadelphuses. The evening primrose *Oenothera missouriensis* seeds itself around the beds and the annual poached-egg flower *Limnanthes douglasii* is grown to cover any bare patches. There are two more exits from this lovely garden. The first leads into the 'Fan' garden – a wedge-shaped space enclosed in yew hedges where box has been planted like the ribs of a fan. A classical statue stands at the meeting point of the ribs and each segment is filled with a block of a single plant. The ornamental grass *Festuca glauca* grows in one, *Santolina virens* (with thread-like leaves) in another and there are colonies of lavender, golden marjoram, thrift, rue, *Alchemilla alpina*, *Anaphalis triplinervis* and a small-leaved variegated hosta.

The second exit leads into the largest enclosure of the garden where there is a swimming-pool and croquet lawn. In recent years the orchard in front of the swimming-pool has been planted with specimen trees. They include a tulip tree

Left: The pool garden on the south side of the house was built on the site of the old tithe barn.

Right: 20-year-old shrub roses and catmint border the path leading to the summer-house designed by Lord Carrington.

(*Liriodendron tulipifera*), a Judas tree (*Cercis siliquastrum*), a golden Indian bean tree (*Catalpa bignonioides* 'Aurea') and the lovely dogwood *Cornus alternifolia* 'Argentea' with its spreading branches and cream and green leaves. A mixed border has been made between the orchard and the croquet lawn. Here buddleias, brooms and hebes have been planted with tamarisk (*Tamarix pentandra*), rugosa roses and philadelphuses. The species clematis *C. flammula* sprawls along the border among the shrubs and clumps of pale salmon-pink poppies and *Iris sibirica*. Two species of the lily-like crinum grow in this border: *C. x powellii* with pink flowers and *C. longifolium* which has flowers striped white and pink.

On the far side of the croquet lawn a wide border has been filled with pink and white flowering plants. There are many roses, white and pink lavender, a variegated iris (*I. pallida variegata*) and the frothy white gypsophila *G. paniculata* 'Bristol Fairy'. A mass of pink and white dianthuses has been planted in the front. The charming China rose *R. chinensis* 'Mutabilis' grows here; it has pointed flame-coloured buds which gradually change colour as they open and are said to resemble butterflies. Here also are the roses 'Little White Pet', 'Natalie Nypels', 'Yvonne Rabier' and the floribunda 'Lilac Charm'. On the wall behind them the attractive *Indigofera gerardiana* grows; it has rose-pink spikes of flowers and elegant pinnate leaves.

From the top of the croquet lawn a path leads to the front of the house where a serpentine wall separates the kitchen garden from the lawn. Shrub roses frame a gate which opens to reveal a long paeony and delphinium border with a stone urn at the far end. This border is another of Lord Carrington's favourite spots. Like the rest of the garden, the kitchen garden is meticulously kept and a wide range of fruit and vegetables is grown although Lord Carrington says he regards

Facing page

Top: A stone urn adds a classical touch to the borders at the centre of the kitchen garden.

Left: Four yews, clipped into decorative shapes, stand at the edge of the lawn to the south of the drive.

Right: A secluded paved garden adjacent to the pool garden where pinks, rock-roses and campanulas grow in the paving.

it as 'an economic folly'.

Across the road from the house Lord Carrington has a second garden which he has been working on for the past five years. He has made it for the whole community to share and has again been helped in its design by Robert Adam. It lies in a dell on both banks of the River Lyde which flows through the village. The scheme has involved scrapping the water-cress beds which used to be there and building a series of pools and 'drops' down the gully. Around the pools and up the slopes of the dell an enormous range of trees and shrubs has been planted The intention has been to create a garden of year-round interest with plants from every continent represented. The effect is lush and exciting.

Lord Carrington is modest about his prowess as a gardener. He claims that his knowledge is scanty compared with that of his wife whom he calls affectionately 'the gardener whose bible is the RHS journal'. While he would love to read more gardening books, he says that he barely has time to skim through *The Economist* – his required reading. When he has time he does read Tony Venison and Christopher Lloyd in *Country Life* and has always found them extremely helpful. A constantly busy life with a great deal of travelling prevents him from visiting other gardens as much as he would like. But there are two that he greatly admires: the one made by Mrs Lancaster at Little Haseley and Garsington Manor made by the Morrells. The Carringtons enjoy swapping plants with other gardeners and make a point of seeking out those plants they have seen and liked in other gardens. Theirs is a garden where someone with a genius for organization has been at work. There is a dominating sense of order and attention to detail – nothing is left to chance. Lord Carrington is dismissive of his own contribution but he is obviously passionately involved at every level. It is undoubtedly another of his successes.

The Lyde Garden was created by Lord Carrington for the enjoyment of the whole community. Plants from all five continents grow here.

129

# Christina Foyle
# in Essex

**A**S ONE MIGHT EXPECT of what were once the grounds of a religious house, the garden at Beeleigh Abbey exudes an air of peace. It belongs to Mr and Mrs Ronald Batty. Mrs Batty is better known as Christina Foyle, the daughter of William Foyle who founded the famous bookshop in Charing Cross Road in London.

The Abbey and its grounds have a long history. It was built in 1189 by the Premonstratensian Order that remained there until the Reformation. There were many owners subsequently until a Colonel Grantham bought it early in this century. He set about restoring the dilapidated building so that today the house consists of the chapter house, the calefactory (in monastic days the only room with a fire) and the dormitory with a secular Tudor addition. It was Colonel Grantham's passion for gardening that led him to plant up the garden as it is today. Sadly he did not live to enjoy it as he was killed in action in 1917. Miss Foyle remembers that when her father bought the house the garden was very overgrown. Being war-time there was no one available to help in it, and so the grass was waist high and weeds obliterated the flower beds. Once the war had ended restoration began, during the course of which a collection of human skulls was dug up. It was William Foyle's custom to secrete them in the car boots of unsuspecting visitors, displaying what his daughter calls his mischievous streak.

Covering 12 acres, the garden's structure is a testament to Colonel Grantham's foresight. All the mature trees and the yew hedges were planted by him. On the south side of the house, a huge flat lawn stretches to the trees which mark the boundary of the garden. A statue of Robert Mantell, the grantor of the land for the building of the Abbey, is its only ornament. At the far western corner a yew arch encloses a bench where, tradition dictates, visitors must sit to make a wish. Grantham's magnificent yew hedge runs the length of the lawn on its eastern side; on its western side a wide herbaceous border is backed by a cherry walk and the orchard. The herbaceous border is planted with a traditional mixture of perennial plants in bold clumps. Cottage garden paeonies, lupins, delphiniums and lady's mantle are mixed with campanulas, pinks, daisies, Jacob's ladder and gypsophila. Near the orchard, adjoining the house, a small sunken garden contains a circular ornamental pool with a fountain; the beds on its perimeter are filled with mixed shrubs and perennials. A large evergreen shrub, *Osmanthus delavayi*, with white sweetly smelling flowers in April, stands beside the path leading from the sunken garden to the house. Near it, in complete contrast, is a golden philadelphus (*P. coronarius* 'Aureus') and a daphne (*D. odora* 'Aureomarginata') which flowers in the late winter and early spring with a rich

The south façade of the abbey seen over a mass of goat's rue (*Galega officinalis*).

fragrance. A small pergola has been erected to screen the 'chicken area' from the sunken garden. Roses, clematises and the lilac 'Michael Buchner' are being trained over it.

On the eastern side of the garden a large wood of broad-leaved trees planted by Colonel Grantham is underplanted with laurels, forsythias, tree paeonies and viburnums. In the spring it comes alive with snowdrops and aconites. A yew walk, its hedges kept clipped to about 4ft, winds through the wood to a seat placed on the bank of the River Blackwater. Between the house and the wood a large rectangular pool covers the site of the monks' chapel. Level greensward surrounds it, fringed with shrubs which merge with the woodland beyond.

From the pool, a walled walk leads to the rose garden which is protected on its western side by Grantham's yew hedge. In this sheltered walk emphasis has been placed on scented plants such as winter and spring flowering viburnums (*V. bodnantense* 'Dawn' and *V. fragrans* in the winter and in the spring *V. carlesii* and the similar but larger *V.* x *burkwoodii* which flowers earlier). There are several mahonias (*M. japonica*, *M.* 'Charity' and *M. aquifolium*) as well as camellias and a small magnolia (*M. stellata*). Miss Foyle's love of lilies is shown with clumps repeated along the border and there are different kinds of euonymus (*E. fortunei radicans* types – 'Silver Pillar', 'Silver Queen' and 'Gold Edge') which provide ground cover at the front of the border. In the spring little reticulata irises are a welcome addition along with scillas and snowdrops. Agapanthus add an exotic touch and delphiniums give height at regular intervals down the border with their soft blue flowers in early June. The wall is covered with climbing plants throughout its length – ivies, honeysuckles, chaenomeles and clematises tumble together, introducing a romantic feel to the garden.

The roses in the large rectangular rose garden are principally HTs and

Left: Mr and Mrs Batty at the calefactory door.

Right: A peacock in the small sunken garden in early spring.

The pure white trumpets of *Lilium candidum* mingle with cerise *Lychnis coronaria* 'Abbotswood Rose' in the border by the rose garden.

floribundas chosen for their scent, with 'Fragrant Cloud', 'Margaret Merrill', 'Scented Air' and 'Miss Harp' among others. At the far end of the rose garden a rustic pergola supports a cascade of roses ('Albertine'), clematises ('Duchess of Edinburgh' and 'Lord Nevill'), philadelphuses ('Virginal') and the early Dutch honeysuckle (*Lonicera periclymenum* 'Belgica'). Between the lawn and the rose garden a wide grassy walk leads back towards the house through a yew arch. Originally the walk was flanked by old mulberry trees but, sadly, some have been lost.

Miss Foyle and her husband are keen conservationists and are happy to share their garden with the wildlife that strays into it from the surrounding farmland. Badgers come every night to feed on scraps left for them outside the calefactory door. They have damaged the lawn but Miss Foyle feels it is a small price to pay for such delightful intruders. Life is always quiet at Beeleigh and while Miss Foyle loves it very much she also enjoys the two days a week she and Mr Batty spend in London running Foyle's.

Preferring order and neatness in her own life Miss Foyle enjoys gardens that are slightly overgrown. 'Masses of honeysuckle framing a door with its blossom scenting the air', is her idea of perfection. She loves all scented plants, particularly lilies, roses, daphnes, philadelphuses and, for their delicate flowers, azaleas and camellias. Ceanothuses and viburnums feature strongly in her list of favourites.

There was a time when the Battys were involved in some of the physical work in the garden but they say now they have to be content to sit and enjoy it on warm sunny days. They feel they are very fortunate to live in such a beautiful place where the formal lines of the yew hedges and lawn and the random planting of the borders make a perfectly harmonious setting for the Abbey.

# Robin Leigh-Pemberton in Kent

ROBIN LEIGH-PEMBERTON, Governor of the Bank of England, believes that the making of honey is 'the extraction from the garden of its finest essence'. He was a farmer and amateur bee-keeper before he became a banker and he still likes to keep in touch with his country roots. There cannot be many people who keep bees in central London, but he does. Two hives have been installed on the roof of his City flat, and he finds that they produce more honey, of a better quality, than do their country cousins at his home, Torry Hill, in Kent.

A spacious house, in the Queen Anne style, Torry Hill was built in 1956 on the site of the Leigh-Pemberton family house. The previous house was big, Victorian and difficult to maintain. It was demolished after the Second World War. The new house stands in magnificent parkland with a commanding view of the River Medway to the east. It took two years to build, and when the Leigh-Pembertons moved in, it was still surrounded by rubble with brambles enveloping what was left of the garden.

Before coming to Torry Hill, Robin Leigh-Pemberton's gardening experience had been limited to looking after a small London garden and taking a 'mild interest' in his mother's garden. With limited knowledge, and a very overgrown garden to get under control, he decided that the only thing to do was to 'push back the frontiers of cultivation gradually', beginning with the area nearest the house. A walled courtyard garden was first made at the back, but this area had been under the old house and the soil was sterile, so tons of topsoil, manure and peat were brought in. Even then it took ten years before the borders looked full and Mr Leigh-Pemberton suspects that the plants will never be really happy. For the central lawn of the walled garden, he laid turf rescued from a grass tennis-court that was being demolished in Sittingbourne. Today, this is a neat and springy square. A narrow terrace, decorated with four statues of cherubs on pedestals, separates the rear of the house from the lawn, and wide flower beds run along the other three sides of the garden. A wide flight of steps faces the terrace from the centre of the north wall opposite. They lead to the old rose garden 12ft above the courtyard. The beds in the walled garden are planted with herbaceous perennials and contain some of Mr Leigh-Pemberton's favourite flowers, especially paeonies. He remembers well some of the first he ordered from Kelway's nursery: 'Sarah Bernhardt', 'Baroness Schroeder', 'Bowl of Beauty' and 'Kelway's Supreme'. He particularly likes 'the dark red cottagey types', and delphiniums and lilies which he grows from seed. He nurtures the seeds of *Lilium regale* and *L. candidum* on the window-sill of his London flat – 'in

Robin Leigh-Pemberton in the
courtyard garden in late
spring.

the interests of economy', he says.

The beds of the courtyard garden contain a spectacular mixture of plants. For colour early in the season there are primulas, lungwort (*Pulmonaria* hybrids) and a golden-flowered spurge, *Euphorbia polychroma*. These are succeeded by columbines, doronicums and the very attractive *Veronica gentianoides* with pale blue-grey spires of flowers until, in high summer, the borders explode with colour. Small violas at the front of the border are backed with oriental poppies, irises, lupins, campanulas, pyrethrums, day lilies, ligularias, herbaceous poten-tillas, delphiniums and swathes of lady's mantle (*Alchemilla mollis*). These borders are punctuated with grey foliage plants such as lamb's ears (*Stachys lanata*), *Lamium maculatum* 'Silver Beacon' with its silver foliage and pink flowers, *Anaphalis triplinervis* and *A. yedoensis*. There are many paeonies and lilies, monkshoods (*Aconitum* hybrids) and agapanthus 'Headbourne' hybrids. Later in the season there is a profusion of sedums and Japanese anemones. At the foot of the steps leading to the rose garden, two stone urns are filled with a mixture of dark red pelargoniums and a tender pink verbena, *V.* x *hybrida* 'Sissinghurst'.

At the top of the steps a hedge of *Berberis* x *stenophylla* separates the courtyard garden from the rose garden which was made in 1930 by Mr Leigh-Pemberton's mother. It was made in the form of an amphitheatre with concentric rings of beds in a square frame. Once the area had been cleared it was replanted with old-fashioned roses. These include the Gallicas – 'Charles de Mills' with crimson flowers and sweet scent and 'Cardinal de Richelieu' with dusky purple flowers. This predominantly red colour scheme is continued with the cerise-red floribunda 'Rosemary Rose' and *Rosa gallica versicolor* with its white-striped crimson flowers. In other beds there is an effective mixture of apricots, yellows and pinks in the flowers of 'Peace', 'Beauty' and, a particular favourite, 'Arthur Hillier' with reddish-pink flowers with a yellow dot in the centre. Round the edge of the amphitheatre is the modern shrub rose, 'Frühlingsgold' with fragrant, pale-yellow flowers early in the season.

After the courtyard and the rose garden, the next essential was a swimming pool and fives court. These now occupy a pavilioned courtyard at the far end of the garden and its walls are decorated with espalier cherries.

The largest single area of the garden is a walled garden of an acre and a half

In the large walled garden, a paved area is surrounded by beds filled with a dazzling selection of herbaceous plants.

A vine-covered pergola stands on one side of the walled garden.

which lies between the rose garden and the swimming pool. This had been a nursery for trees during the war and, as a result, the soil was rather impoverished. As a silver wedding present to her husband Mrs Leigh-Pemberton called in the firm of Waterers to redesign this part of the garden. They were given a list of likes and dislikes and specific requirements such as the provision of plants particularly rich in nectar for the bees, a manageable alpine garden for Mrs Leigh-Pemberton and a general emphasis on shrubs for ease of maintenance. All the ground inside the walls was ploughed and levelled and tons of manure were dug in to recondition the soil. Quantities of York paving for the paths, an acre of turf and thousands of plants were then brought in by Waterers. Today this garden is developing into a place of rich variety. The walls are covered with clematises, escallonias, honeysuckles, roses, ceanothuses and a magnificent Moroccan broom (*Cytisus battandieri*) with its pineapple-scented yellow flowers. On three sides the borders have curved corners to soften their lines and are planted with a mass of shrubs – roses, spiraeas, weigelas, hebes, brooms, lilacs and hibiscuses. Among the weigelas is the rare and beautiful *W. middendorffiana* with large buff-yellow flowers early in the season. Winter structure is provided by such evergreens as osmanthus (both *O. heterophylla* and *O. delavayi*), mahonias, viburnums, escallonias and the ornamental *Garrya elliptica*. Scent in different seasons is given by a collection of daphnes – the early spring flowering *D. odora* 'Aureo-marginata' with cream-margined leaves, *D.* x *burkwoodii* 'Somerset' with pale pink flowers in late spring and the pink-purple flowered *D. mezereum*. Among the less common shrubs are *Exochorda* x *macrantha* 'The Bride', with snow-white flowers in late spring, and the lovely Chinese dogwood *Cornus kousa* with its slender, creamy bracts.

The fourth side of this new garden is paved. Two rectangular beds contain Mrs Leigh-Pemberton's collection of alpines and a small bed near the entrance to the rose garden has herbs. A vine-covered pergola provides shade for troughs containing more alpines and succulents. Double rectangular beds lie in front of the pergola and others edge the paved area. They are overflowing with perennials. A York-stone path cuts across the lawn to a small pool set in its own paved circle, beside which are seats backed with beds that are full of colour. All the plants in these beds are strikingly well tended by the Leigh-Pemberton's head-gardener and his assistant. Herbaceous plants are supported by hazel twigs which are collected from the woods each autumn. Their size is carefully judged

Facing page: A stunning collection of perennials in the walled garden –*Alstroemeria ligtu* hybrids and spires of white delphiniums in the foreground. The boldness of the planting suits the great size of the enclosure.

The walled garden was laid out as a silver wedding present from Mrs Leigh-Pemberton to her husband.

Mr Leigh-Pemberton's mother made the rose garden in the 1930s but it has since been replanted. The floribunda rose 'Iceberg' is in the foreground.

so that they are soon concealed by the leaves of the growing plants. It is the kind of detail, so rarely seen today, that transforms a herbaceous border.

In the spring, the entrance drive on the west side of the house is edged with thousands of naturalised daffodils. Miraculously, they survived being flattened by heavy vehicles when the previous house was used as an army headquarters in the war. In the park, Mr Leigh-Pemberton has added to the many mature trees which were there when he came, some of which were planted in the early 19th century. To the magnificent chestnuts, cedars and acacias, he has added a beech avenue and varieties of flowering cherries whose blossom forms a canopy over the daffodils in their season. Broad walks are cut through the long grass as Mr Leigh-Pemberton likes the contrast of the different lengths and wants to encourage the wild flowers to seed themselves. Between the drive and the rose garden shrubberies of rhododendrons and azaleas seem to flourish in the soil of clay over chalk.

Mr Leigh-Pemberton regrets that he is unable to give enough time to his garden at weekends. Each August, during his annual holiday, he compensates by concentrating on a single project. In 1985, he extended the lawn to the north-east of the house and, to make a focal point, introduced specimen maples at the far end. The south-west wind is troublesome here, particularly to the rhododendrons, and he intends to increase screen planting to protect them. An enormous amount of leaf-mould is used to feed the rhododendrons and azaleas. His next project is to turn part of the paddock on the east side of the house into a wild-flower lawn. In the past he has tried to raise white daffodils and bluebells from seed – but without success. He now proposes to plough the area and sow it with sackfuls of wild-flower seed.

Mr Leigh-Pemberton cares deeply about conservation – both on his farm and in his garden. He won a prize recently for the best methods of combining conservation of the countryside with efficient farming. In spite of having little time to read gardening books he has acquired a wide and practical knowledge. He sees gardening as both a recreation and a creative outlet but says modestly, 'The garden has simply grown on us.' He also enjoys visiting gardens abroad but finds they 'only whet the appetite for returning to one's own'.

High brick walls protect tender species within the enclosed garden.

# Bryan Forbes
# in Surrey

TO BRYAN FORBES gardening is all about 'trial and error and heartache'. His interest began nearly 30 years ago when he and his wife, Nanette Newman, moved to Virginia Water in Surrey. They thought the 1930s house looked 'like a biscuit factory' when they first saw it, but its situation on the edge of the Wentworth Estate was peaceful and its overgrown 14-acre garden stunningly beautiful. The resident squirrels were so unused to human company they would eat straight from the hand. For two impecunious actors the purchase was a huge financial undertaking and all their resources and energies went into making the house habitable. Mr Forbes regrets not starting on the garden much sooner than they were able. 'You have to wait so long with trees. Someone will get the benefit of this garden in 20 years.'

Born a Cockney and brought up in London, he came to the garden with no previous knowledge but with a great love of the land acquired on his grandparents' farm in Lincolnshire. Learning as he went along, he considers his garden is 'thrown together and wild'. An informal glade of silver birch, oak, sycamore and gigantic pines mark the approach to the house. Against a background of 60-year-old species rhododendrons near the house, island shrubberies of azaleas, hybrid rhododendrons and *Pieris formosa* var. *forrestii* soften a group of towering chestnuts and in early summer their blossom explodes upon the scene. Although some of the rhododendron shrubberies existed when the Forbeses came here, they have constantly been added to and now have the appearance of luxuriant maturity.

Behind the house in a corner of the garden a double row of beeches arch towards each other, forming a vast vaulted tunnel. They line the remains of the carriage drive to old Wentworth House. This part of the garden is perhaps Mr Forbes's favourite, but has been the source of some pain as well as pleasure. Recently a freak 120mph wind uprooted two of the 400-year-old trees, 'plucking them out like teeth'. It is just the sort of unpredictable act of nature that Mr Forbes finds depressing. A walled garden built by Mr Forbes stands beside the drive. This no longer belongs to him but set into its outer face he has placed busts of the Four Seasons which he found over the years in junk yards. It is a very effective way of ornamenting an otherwise rather blank wall.

To the west of the house the lands falls away sharply, forming a steep ridge. When the garden was originally created Westmorland stone was 'poured' down from the top to form an enormous rockery. By 1957 it had become totally obscured by undergrowth. Today its massive stones form the framework for all the huge azaleas, heathers, ferns, brooms and Japanese maples found there.

A dazzling water-fall of azaleas
plunges down the rockery
below the house.

Bryan Forbes on the steps of the gypsy caravan given to his daughters by Sir John and Lady Mills. It now stands beneath a Norway maple close to the ornamental pool.

Below this, in the valley, an irregularly-shaped lake is framed by woods bordering the Wentworth Golf Club and by all kinds of specimen trees planted by Mr Forbes.

On the lawn near the house is an ornamental pool with a fountain. A fine weeping pear (*Pyrus salicifolia* 'Pendula') stands beside it. Three false acacias (*Robinia pseudacacia* 'Frisia') were planted on the lawn 15 years ago to lighten a dark corner. Their yellowy-green leaves contrast beautifully with the dark leathery-leaved rhododendrons behind. Beverley Nichols used to come and advise about the garden – 'Always plant trees in juxtaposition,' he said. It is advice that Mr Forbes has tried to follow. Across the lawn, near the rockery, he has placed a large bust of Napoleon on a plinth. It is swathed with the climbing form of one of the best of the Bourbon roses, 'Souvenir de la Malmaison' – 'I thought it rather fitting,' he says.

Restoration of the garden has been a long, slow process. It was completely covered with a jungle of trees, saplings and weeds when the Forbeses arrived. 7,000 saplings were removed to provide sufficient light and space for the more mature trees and shrubs and to make space for a lawn. Once the clearing was finished, Mr Forbes began planting, but with mixed success. The garden lies on Bagshot sand with an iron pan stratum beneath, producing difficult soil, where rhododendrons, azaleas and maples do well but roses fare very badly. However Mr Forbes perseveres with roses although they have to be replaced every three years. Overcrowding remains a problem as permission is required to remove any tree with a trunk diameter of more than six inches. Seven large pines were removed from the middle of the lawn once it had been established that they were a danger. Mr Forbes has had to undertake to plant three trees for every one removed, a commitment of which he approves as it has always been his policy to replace common trees with more interesting specimens. For the last 19 years, he has been helped by Richard Smith, his full-time gardener, whose contribution to

144

Left: An aviary designed by Lord Snowdon stands on the far side of the lawn.

Right: Mr Forbes has been adept at finding garden ornaments in junk yards. Here, in a peaceful corner of the garden, an ornate cast-iron seat by the pool is shaded by a weeping pear.

restoring the garden has been invaluable.

Mr Forbes likes gardens to be wild and dramatic. Immaculate lawns are not for him – 'a bore' he calls them. He much prefers to throw wild flower seeds over his to create a meadow effect. He likes to see the garden inhabited by wildlife – there are often visiting swans on the lake and foxes and badgers make tracks across the lawn. As a keen conservationist it worries him that with England's finite amount of land, still not enough importance is attached to its preservation and use. If it were possible he would like to be a politician running a 'Ministry of Taste', but only so long as it had dictatorial powers! He would love to be 'miles away from anything' but is too much of realist to be a farmer.

Planting trees over such a long period has given Mr Forbes the opportunity to decide which he likes most and which do well in his garden. His interest has become so well known that his friends call him 'Capability' Forbes. Maples are particular favourites. An enormous Norway maple (*Acer platanoides*) casts its shade over the drive and a restored gypsy caravan. Near the terrace which surrounds the house he planted a snake-bark maple (*Acer grosseri* var. *hersii*) several years ago. It is now 15ft tall with exquisitely marked bark – olive-green striped with white. Another unusual snake-bark maple, *Acer capillipes*, planted in the lawn, has brown bark striped with white and red-orange foliage in the autumn. Across the lawn an aviary designed by Lord Snowdon is home to Mr Forbes's Barbary doves. Nearby stands a splendid sycamore, *Acer pseudoplatanus* 'Brilliantissimum'. In the spring its leaves are shrimp pink becoming pale yellow-green and finally green as the season goes on. On the birth of each of his daughters over 20 years ago Mr Forbes planted a *Magnolia* x *soulangiana* 'Lennei' on the lawn beyond the terrace. Now these magnificent spreading specimens flower freely every May. One of a pair of weeping elms (*Ulmus glabra* 'Pendula'), planted as sentinels at the end of the terrace, has died and has been replaced by another favourite, a weeping pear. The rockery contains many Japanese maples which grow slowly and remain fairly small. Well represented are the deservedly popular *Acer palmatum* 'Atropurpureum' with crimson leaves all through the summer, *A.p.* 'Dissectum' and *A.p.* 'Dissectum Atropurpureum' with their finely cut, delicate foliage.

The large-scale landscaping project has caused some anxiety. The valley below the rockery used to be extremely boggy. It was decided that the creation of a lake would solve this problem. Unfortunately, during excavation work the contractors piled up the dredged soil indiscriminately around the existing trees and the acidity promptly killed them. Later, the addition of tons of hop compost neutralised the soil but iron deposits in the lake bed coloured the water brown. Feeding the lake is a sluggish stream which runs down the valley from behind the house. If he had inexhaustible funds, Mr Forbes would like to build a cascade down the valley, increasing the flow and recycling the water via a pumping system. The raised banks have provided more ground for planting. There was a group of sweet gums (*Liquidambar styraciflua*) already planted on the far side of the lake; it is likely that these beautiful trees are some of the largest specimens in England. In the autumn their foliage turns crimson, red, purple and gold, making a startling focus of colour. A mature Arizona cypress (*Cupressus glabra*) contrasts well with a weeping silver birch (*Betula pendula*). Both were transplanted here as self-sown seedlings, as were many of the trees in the garden. A red oak (*Quercus rubra*) planted seven years ago, has grown enormously and is encroaching on a plantation of aspens (*Populus tremula*),

The rockery below the house was retrieved from the undergrowth. A wide selection of plants has been added since, including the spectacular azaleas.

whose leaves shimmer silver in the sunlight.

Although trees are his principal interest, Mr Forbes would love to grow roses successfully, particularly those with a scent. He is fond of 'old-fashioned' flowers such as hollyhocks, sunflowers and paeonies and the border around the terrace is full of delphiniums. Mrs Forbes is not a keen gardener but does enjoy looking after the pots on the terrace. With his wide interests, Mr Forbes feels he has been lucky to have been able to pursue more than one career. He is a man of formidable energy. Having been an actor, a film director and a bookseller, he now spends a good deal of time writing novels. He finds the garden a solace when he is depressed or has writer's block. 'It's so comforting just to walk around and take in the trees, flowers and wildlife.'

Friends, and friends' gardens, have influenced him in the management of his own. Dame Edith Evans had a lovely garden in Kent which he would like to emulate. 'She had such wonderful roses,' he says wistfully. Sissinghurst and Nymans have also inspired him and provided good ideas – as has Roddy Llewellyn who is well versed in 'all those Latin names', says Mr Forbes, 'when all I want to know is if a thing will live.' Mr Forbes's gardening philosophy has evolved over the 30 years of running his garden. He has had to learn to wait and be patient. 'I never uproot anything precious even if it looks as if it's given up the ghost. You never know with trees – they may do nothing for seven years and then shoot.' Although he professes to being a frustrated gardener, to the onlooker the garden reveals only his success.

Left: To the east of the house the woods have been reclaimed and replanted.

Right: The lake in the valley is surrounded by fine specimen trees, seen here from the terrace above the rockery.

# Sir John Rothenstein in Oxfordshire

*I*T WAS PURE CHANCE THAT LED Sir John Rothenstein, a former Director of the Tate Gallery, to give up living in London and buy a house in Oxfordshire in 1947. During the war he and his wife were living above the gallery. Concerned about the possibility of fire destroying the building, he never left it for the safety of an air-raid shelter. To give them a rest, friends offered to put the Rothensteins up at their house in Newington in Oxfordshire. They loved the countryside and decided to look for a house there. They were lucky enough to find a spacious Georgian rectory with a wilderness of a garden.

Beauforest House dates from 1500 but the largest existing part was built between 1795 and 1805 by a parson called Charles Moss. He was a rich cleric – 'an Anglican disgrace', the Rothensteins call him. Fortunately he used some of his money to enlarge Beauforest House and to lay out the garden, the remnants of which survive today. When the Rothensteins moved in, however, they were faced with a jungle which needed a hatchet to cut through it. They were on the point of giving up when they fortunately met Father Vincent Thomas, a Jesuit theologian at Oxford, who offered to help them. It was the beginning of a deep friendship and a gardening partnership that has, over 35 years, produced a gem of a garden.

Beautifully situated on one bank of the River Thame, the garden is a subtle blend of formality and informality. It covers three acres and lies principally to the north and west of the house with the river forming the western boundary. An extensive lawn slopes gently from the house to the river, with informal plantings of trees and shrubs. To the east of the house the drive is shaded by a huge chestnut tree believed to have been planted in 1880. It dominates a small garden hidden behind the house. On the paved area outside the back door a collection of hydrangeas and house-leeks grows in pots. The wall behind is smothered with plants including a huge *Magnolia grandiflora* 'Exmouth'. Its largest companion is a *Vitis coignetiae* which has been invaded by a wisteria and the yellow clematis *C. tangutica*. In the bed below the climbers there is a simple but effective planting of bergenias, plume poppies and lady's mantle. On the far side of the small lawn a semi-circular border contains an informal assortment of roses, shrubs and perennials.

A flat lawn lies to the north of the house. On its west side, where the ground begins to slope down to the river, there is a massive yew – the largest tree in the garden. Concealed below its widely-spreading branches there is a very old mulberry tree. Nearby, five Irish yews mark the entrance to the formal garden to the north. When the Rothensteins arrived they decided to cut off the tops to

Sir John and Lady Rothenstein
amidst the topiary of their
unique garden.

produce their attractive columnar shape. On the east of the flat lawn, a wide curved bed has been planted with some favourite shrubs and perennials. Its two tallest plants are a pair of *Cornus kousa*, a graceful dogwood which produces its flower-like bracts in June. Together with green and purple smoke bushes (*Cotinus coggygria* and *C.c.* 'Foliis Purpureis') and the golden spiraea (*S.* x *bumalda* 'Gold Flame') they make an effective backdrop for the lilies, paeonies, foxgloves and roses planted in front. The roses here are old and new. The new are represented by the modern shrub rose 'Fritz Nobis' with its vivid pink flowers, and the old by what Lady Rothenstein calls 'Lesser Maiden's Blush' – a form of the ancient Alba rose 'Maiden's Blush' – with the most delicate of pink flowers. It was discovered in the undergrowth when the garden was cleared and has continued to seed itself throughout the garden. This rose was identified by Graham Stuart Thomas but the identity of another rose found at Beauforest has baffled him. It has distinctly quartered blooms in subtle shades of dark pink and, for want of a better name, it is referred to as 'the Beauforest rose'. To the east of this curved bed a sturdy pergola has replaced an older one. A white wisteria grows over it, with *Vitis coignetiae*, hybrid clematises and another 'Lesser Maiden's Blush'. The pergola leads to a nut walk which the Rothensteins believe was planted in Victorian times. Its two lines of hazel trees lean towards each other creating a sun-dappled tunnel. An ornamental oil-storage jar on a plinth smothered with *Clematis montana* stands at its far end. Father Vincent saw the oil jar in a sale at Heal's a few years ago and bought it for £8; a judicious buy, he feels, and the perfect focal point for the walk.

When work was started on the garden the area beyond the Irish yews was a wilderness. It took years to tame it; in fact Lady Rothenstein says the recent history of the garden could be summed up as 'clearing, clearing and more clearing'. Sir John made himself responsible for ridding the garden of thistles and nettles, removing mountains of them over the years. The Rothensteins were delighted to discover traces of a formal garden here, namely some old box hedges arranged in parallel lines forming a cross. These may date from Charles Moss's time and have been preserved. Although not complete, the lines effectively divide this part of the garden into four rectangular segments. At the axis of the

hedges a wrought-iron gazebo on stone pillars makes a stunning centre-piece. The idea for this came from one Lady Rothenstein remembers, built by her grandfather for the family home in Kentucky.

The Rothensteins believe that a garden tells you 'what you need where' and this seemed to be the perfect spot to grow old roses, which they love. The roses are scattered informally about three of the box segments, accompanied by shrubs, perennials and herbs. There is a wide selection, but the Gallica 'Charles de Mills' is still a firm favourite, with its strong scent and rich crimson flowers made up of masses of tiny petals. In complete contrast is the HT 'Tranquillity' which Lady Rothenstein regards as having 'the most perfect buds'. Bourbons are well represented – 'Madame Pierre Oger', 'Madame Isaac Péreire' and 'La Reine Victoria' – with the Hybrid Perpetuals 'Souvenir du Docteur Jamain' and 'Ferdinand Pichard' which are not only beautiful but flower over a long period and have a range of exotic scents. Several Albas grow here – the exquisite 'Celestial', 'Queen of Denmark' and the ubiquitous 'Lesser Maiden's Blush'. All are renowned for their delicate beauty which belies their hardiness. A group of Gallicas include 'Cardinal de Richelieu' with dark purple flowers, 'Empress Josephine' – a clear pink with a darker vein – and the much-loved *Rosa gallica versicolor*. At one time there were traditional herbaceous borders in two of the segments but they were never satisfactory and today the roses are accompanied by many shrubs – berberises, spiraeas, hibiscuses, philadelphuses and the lovely Russian paeony *Paeonia mlokosewitschii* with its large single flowers of clear yellow. Within this framework are many perennials – wormwood, campanulas, phloxes, day lilies, sedums and goat's rue.

The fourth segment has been paved. Fan-shaped beds surround a stone

Left: Throughout the garden ornaments are skilfully used to complement the planting and add romantic touches.

Right: A curved border leads to the Irish yews at the entrance to the topiary garden. The rose 'Lesser Maiden's Blush' can be seen underneath *Cornus kousa*.

A blue spruce (*Picea pungens* 'Hoopsii') grown in a lead urn among a variety of shrubs and perennials in the inner garden.

bird-bath in the centre. Here the emphasis is on topiary in miniature with a delightful arrangement of clipped domes of green and variegated box, *Euonymus fortunei radicans* 'Gold Finger' and four golden yews. There are stone pillars along two sides of the paved area with heavy rope suspended between them. Clematises, ivies and climbing roses grow up the pillars and along the ropes. More shrub roses grow among the clipped domes with herbs at their feet – a deliciously scented profusion of golden marjoram, lavender, rue and purple sage with masses of catmint and santolina. This small area has a character of restrained formality which blends beautifully with the rest of this exquisite garden-within-a-garden.

At the far end of the box hedges, a hedge of hawthorn and beech separates this part of the garden from a small lawn beyond. A rustic fence, lavishly draped with the climbing rose 'Albéric Barbier', marks the edge of the orchard beyond the lawn.

There used to be great elms in the orchard but they were lost after a long battle with Dutch elm disease. However, their demise has made room for other trees. There is the winter-flowering cherry *Prunus subhirtella* 'Autumnalis' which can flower more or less continuously from November to March. Here too is the lovely early-flowering *Prunus incisa*. Two other good cherries are *Prunus serrulata* 'Shirofugen' with double white flowers and *Prunus sargentii* with single pink flowers, decorative dark brown bark and good autumn colour. Beside these are two ornamental birches – the weeping silver birch *Betula pendula* 'Youngii' and the white-barked Himalayan birch *B. jacquemontii*.

The broad sweep of grass stretching along the river bank from the orchard to the house provides a splendid setting for carefully chosen specimen trees, where

they are seen to their best advantage above the slow waters of the River Thame. A *Liquidambar styraciflua* has not, however, lived up to expectations as its leaves do not become crimson in the autumn. A poplar, *Populus candicans* 'Aurora', is planted near the water where its variegated leaves stand out against the alders beyond. Surprisingly, willows do not generally do well here but there is a fine specimen of a weeping willow (*Salix babylonica*) . A favourite willow (*Salix* x *sepulcralis*) had to be removed when it became diseased but Lady Rothenstein is determined to replace it with a Peking willow (*S. matsudana*). Below the house, near the river bank, there is a canoe birch (*Betula papyrifera*) and a mature Ohio buckeye (*Aesculus glabra*) – both much-loved trees that were planted to remind Lady Rothenstein of her childhood in Kentucky.

To the west of the house there is a Lutyens-style summerhouse and terrace overlooking the river. An enormous weeping beech (*Fagus sylvatica* 'Pendula') was planted in front of the terrace about twenty years ago and, although it partly blocks the view, it helps to protect the terrace from the winds that blow across the river.

Writing has always been a passion of Sir John's. He has published over thirty books and is still writing. He says he has a conscience about getting his thoughts on paper. His quota of 500 words a day is 'like cream on milk – it will go sour if not skimmed.' He finds the garden has always been a solace. Since his retirement he walks in it every day – 'it is my greatest joy'. The Rothensteins and Father Vincent look upon the garden as a cooperative enterprise. They say their most valuable lesson has been that 'One learns through bitter disappointment that nature has to be respected.' Quoting one of his favourite painters, Francis Bacon, Sir John adds 'But the art comes in exploiting the accidents.'

Left: When in flood the River Thame reaches the foot of these steps.

Right: Old box hedges divide the inner garden into segments – at the centre an elegant 'pagoda'.

Facing page: The nut walk planted in the 19th century.

154

# *Index*

Note: References in *italic* refer to illustrations.